Wine Tasting
Journal

Copyright © 2019 Ramini Brands

"Wine is one of the most civilized things in the world and one of the most natural things of the world that has been brought to the greatest perfection, and it offers a greater range for enjoyment and appreciation than, possibly, any other purely sensory thing."

~Ernest Hemingway

Index

Wine Tasting Journey

Page	Wine I Tasted	Location

Index

Wine Tasting Journey

Page	Wine I Tasted	Location

Index

Wine Tasting Journey

Page	Wine I Tasted	Location

Index

Wine Tasting Journey

Page	Wine I Tasted	Location

Index

Wine Tasting Journey

Page	Wine I Tasted	Location

Index

Wine Tasting Journey

Page	Wine I Tasted	Location

Index

Wine Tasting Journey

Page	Wine I Tasted	Location

Index

Wine Tasting Journey

Page	Wine I Tasted	Location

Index

Wine Tasting Journey

Page	Wine I Tasted	Location

Index

Wine Tasting Journey

Page	Wine I Tasted	Location

WINE: Pinot Gris Vintage: 2015 Producer: River Road
Region/Country: Sonoma County Price: $9.00 Date Tasted: 6/14/19

Grape(s): _____

Importer/Distributor: _____ Alcohol % 12.9%

Circle Your Ratings Below

Color/Style: Red (White) Rose Sparkling Effervescent Fortified
Appearance: (Thin) Translucent Saturated Opaque
Dry/Sweet Spectrum: Dry 1 2 (3) 4 5 6 7 8 9 10 Sweet
Body: (Light) Light-Medium Medium Medium-Full Full
Balance: Unbalanced 1 2 3 4 5 6 (7) 8 9 10 Balanced
Finish: (Short) Short-Medium Medium Medium-Long Long
Tasting Experience: Poor 1 2 3 4 5 6 7 8 (9) 10 Excellent
Price-to-Value Ratio: Poor 1 2 3 4 5 6 7 8 9 (10) Excellent

Smell

☐ TOAST	☐ COFFEE	☐ CITRUS	☐ HONEY
☐ TOBACCO	☐ SMOKE	☐ MELON	☐ APPLES
☐ LEATHER	☐ PEPPER	☐ OAK	☐ TROPICAL FRUITS
☐ MUSHROOM	☐ MINT	☐ BERRIES	☐ GRASS
☐ JAM	☐ SPICE	☐ NUTMEG	☐ FLORAL
☐ CHOCOLATE	☐ ALMOND	☐ VEGETAL	☒ Clean

Taste

☐ DARK FRUITS	☐ EARTH	☐ TOAST	☐ NUTMEG
☐ BERRIES	☐ PEPPER	☐ GRASS	☐ VEGETAL
☐ PLUMS	☐ VANILLA	☐ CITRUS	☐ FLORAL
☐ MUSHROOM	☐ COFFEE	☐ MELON	☐ HONEY
☐ TOBACCO	☐ LICORICE	☐ LYCHEE	☒ PEARS
☐ CHOCOLATE	☐ LEATHER	☐ ALMOND	☒ PEACHES

Green Apple

WINE: Chablis Vintage: 2017 Producer: Domaine Chenevieres
Region/Country: Burgandy, France Price: 30.00 Date Tasted: 6/15/19
Grape(s): Chardonnay

Importer/Distributor: _____ Alcohol % 13 %

Circle Your Ratings Below

Color/Style: Red (White) Rose Sparkling Effervescent Fortified
Appearance: (Thin) Translucent Saturated Opaque
Dry/Sweet Spectrum: Dry 1 2 (3) 4 5 6 7 8 9 10 Sweet
Body: (Light) Light-Medium Medium Medium-Full Full
Balance: Unbalanced 1 2 3 4 5 6 7 (8) 9 10 Balanced
Finish: (Short) Short-Medium Medium Medium-Long Long
Tasting Experience: Poor 1 2 3 4 5 6 7 8 9 (10) Excellent
Price-to-Value Ratio: Poor 1 2 3 4 5 6 7 (8) 9 10 Excellent

Smell

☐ TOAST	☐ COFFEE	☐ CITRUS	☐ HONEY
☐ TOBACCO	☐ SMOKE	☐ MELON	☒ APPLES
☐ LEATHER	☐ PEPPER	☐ OAK	☐ TROPICAL FRUITS
☐ MUSHROOM	☐ MINT	☐ BERRIES	☐ GRASS
☐ JAM	☐ SPICE	☐ NUTMEG	☐ FLORAL
☐ CHOCOLATE	☐ ALMOND	☐ VEGETAL	☐ _____

Taste

☐ DARK FRUITS	☐ EARTH	☐ TOAST	☐ NUTMEG
☐ BERRIES	☐ PEPPER	☐ GRASS	☐ VEGETAL
☐ PLUMS	☐ VANILLA	☐ CITRUS	☐ FLORAL
☐ MUSHROOM	☐ COFFEE	☐ MELON	☐ HONEY
☐ TOBACCO	☐ LICORICE	☐ LYCHEE	☒ PEARS
☐ CHOCOLATE	☐ LEATHER	☐ ALMOND	☐ PEACHES

14

WINE: Sandgrube Vintage: 2018 Producer:

Region/Country: Danube River Austria Price: 30⁰⁰ Date Tasted: 6/15/19

Grape(s): Gruner Veltliner

Importer/Distributor: _____ Alcohol % 12.5%

Circle Your Ratings Below

Color/Style: Red (White) Rose Sparkling Effervescent Fortified
Appearance: (Thin) Translucent Saturated Opaque
Dry/Sweet Spectrum: Dry 1 2 (3) 4 5 6 7 8 9 10 Sweet
Body: (Light) Light-Medium Medium Medium-Full Full
Balance: Unbalanced 1 2 3 4 (5) 6 7 8 9 10 Balanced
Finish: Short Short-Medium Medium Medium-Long Long
Tasting Experience: Poor 1 2 3 4 5 6 7 8 9 (10) Excellent
Price-to-Value Ratio: Poor 1 2 3 4 5 6 7 (8) 9 10 Excellent

Smell

☐ TOAST	☐ COFFEE	☐ CITRUS	☐ HONEY
☐ TOBACCO	☐ SMOKE	☐ MELON	☐ APPLES
☐ LEATHER	☐ PEPPER	☐ OAK	☐ TROPICAL FRUITS
☐ MUSHROOM	☐ MINT	☐ BERRIES	☐ GRASS
☐ JAM	☐ SPICE	☐ NUTMEG	☐ FLORAL
☐ CHOCOLATE	☐ ALMOND	☐ VEGETAL	☐ _____

Taste

☐ DARK FRUITS	☐ EARTH	☐ TOAST	☐ NUTMEG
☐ BERRIES	☐ PEPPER	☐ GRASS	☐ VEGETAL
☐ PLUMS	☐ VANILLA	☐ CITRUS	☐ FLORAL
☐ MUSHROOM	☐ COFFEE	☐ MELON	☐ HONEY
☐ TOBACCO	☐ LICORICE	☐ LYCHEE	☐ PEARS
☐ CHOCOLATE	☐ LEATHER	☐ ALMOND	☐ PEACHES

15

Circle Your Ratings Below

Color/Style: Red   White   Rose   Sparkling   Effervescent   Fortified

Appearance: Thin   Translucent   Saturated   Opaque

Dry/Sweet Spectrum: Dry 1 2 3 4 5 6 7 8 9 10 Sweet

Body: Light   Light-Medium   Medium   Medium-Full   Full

Balance: Unbalanced 1 2 3 4 5 6 7 8 9 10 Balanced

Finish: Short   Short-Medium   Medium   Medium-Long   Long

Tasting Experience: Poor 1 2 3 4 5 6 7 8 9 10 Excellent

Price-to-Value Ratio: Poor 1 2 3 4 5 6 7 8 9 10 Excellent

Smell

☐ TOAST	☐ COFFEE	☐ CITRUS	☐ HONEY
☐ TOBACCO	☐ SMOKE	☐ MELON	☐ APPLES
☐ LEATHER	☐ PEPPER	☐ OAK	☐ TROPICAL FRUITS
☐ MUSHROOM	☐ MINT	☐ BERRIES	☐ GRASS
☐ JAM	☐ SPICE	☐ NUTMEG	☐ FLORAL
☐ CHOCOLATE	☐ ALMOND	☐ VEGETAL	☐ _____

Taste

☐ DARK FRUITS	☐ EARTH	☐ TOAST	☐ NUTMEG
☐ BERRIES	☐ PEPPER	☐ GRASS	☐ VEGETAL
☐ PLUMS	☐ VANILLA	☐ CITRUS	☐ FLORAL
☐ MUSHROOM	☐ COFFEE	☐ MELON	☐ HONEY
☐ TOBACCO	☐ LICORICE	☐ LYCHEE	☐ PEARS
☐ CHOCOLATE	☐ LEATHER	☐ ALMOND	☐ PEACHES

WINE: _____ Vintage: _____ Producer: _____

Region/Country: _____ Price: _____ Date Tasted: _____

Grape(s): _____

Importer/Distributor: _____ Alcohol % _____

Circle Your Ratings Below

Color/Style: Red   White   Rose   Sparkling   Effervescent   Fortified
Appearance: Thin   Translucent   Saturated   Opaque
Dry/Sweet Spectrum: Dry 1 2 3 4 5 6 7 8 9 10 Sweet
Body: Light   Light-Medium   Medium   Medium-Full   Full
Balance: Unbalanced 1 2 3 4 5 6 7 8 9 10 Balanced
Finish: Short   Short-Medium   Medium   Medium-Long   Long
Tasting Experience: Poor   1 2 3 4 5 6 7 8 9 10 Excellent
Price-to-Value Ratio: Poor   1 2 3 4 5 6 7 8 9 10 Excellent

Smell

☐ TOAST	☐ COFFEE	☐ CITRUS	☐ HONEY
☐ TOBACCO	☐ SMOKE	☐ MELON	☐ APPLES
☐ LEATHER	☐ PEPPER	☐ OAK	☐ TROPICAL FRUITS
☐ MUSHROOM	☐ MINT	☐ BERRIES	☐ GRASS
☐ JAM	☐ SPICE	☐ NUTMEG	☐ FLORAL
☐ CHOCOLATE	☐ ALMOND	☐ VEGETAL	☐ _____

Taste

☐ DARK FRUITS	☐ EARTH	☐ TOAST	☐ NUTMEG
☐ BERRIES	☐ PEPPER	☐ GRASS	☐ VEGETAL
☐ PLUMS	☐ VANILLA	☐ CITRUS	☐ FLORAL
☐ MUSHROOM	☐ COFFEE	☐ MELON	☐ HONEY
☐ TOBACCO	☐ LICORICE	☐ LYCHEE	☐ PEARS
☐ CHOCOLATE	☐ LEATHER	☐ ALMOND	☐ PEACHES

WINE: _____ Vintage: _____ Producer: _____

Region/Country: _____ Price: _____ Date Tasted: _____

Grape(s): _____

Importer/Distributor: _____ Alcohol % _____

Circle Your Ratings Below

Color/Style: Red White Rose Sparkling Effervescent Fortified
Appearance: Thin Translucent Saturated Opaque
Dry/Sweet Spectrum: Dry 1 2 3 4 5 6 7 8 9 10 Sweet
Body: Light Light-Medium Medium Medium-Full Full
Balance: Unbalanced 1 2 3 4 5 6 7 8 9 10 Balanced
Finish: Short Short-Medium Medium Medium-Long Long
Tasting Experience: Poor 1 2 3 4 5 6 7 8 9 10 Excellent
Price-to-Value Ratio: Poor 1 2 3 4 5 6 7 8 9 10 Excellent

Smell

☐ TOAST	☐ COFFEE	☐ CITRUS	☐ HONEY
☐ TOBACCO	☐ SMOKE	☐ MELON	☐ APPLES
☐ LEATHER	☐ PEPPER	☐ OAK	☐ TROPICAL FRUITS
☐ MUSHROOM	☐ MINT	☐ BERRIES	☐ GRASS
☐ JAM	☐ SPICE	☐ NUTMEG	☐ FLORAL
☐ CHOCOLATE	☐ ALMOND	☐ VEGETAL	☐ _____

Taste

☐ DARK FRUITS	☐ EARTH	☐ TOAST	☐ NUTMEG
☐ BERRIES	☐ PEPPER	☐ GRASS	☐ VEGETAL
☐ PLUMS	☐ VANILLA	☐ CITRUS	☐ FLORAL
☐ MUSHROOM	☐ COFFEE	☐ MELON	☐ HONEY
☐ TOBACCO	☐ LICORICE	☐ LYCHEE	☐ PEARS
☐ CHOCOLATE	☐ LEATHER	☐ ALMOND	☐ PEACHES

WINE: _____ Vintage: _____ Producer: _____

Region/Country: _____ Price: _____ Date Tasted: _____

Grape(s): _____

Importer/Distributor: _____ Alcohol % _____

Circle Your Ratings Below

Color/Style: Red   White   Rose   Sparkling   Effervescent   Fortified

Appearance: Thin   Translucent   Saturated   Opaque

Dry/Sweet Spectrum: Dry 1 2 3 4 5 6 7 8 9 10 Sweet

Body: Light   Light-Medium   Medium   Medium-Full   Full

Balance: Unbalanced 1 2 3 4 5 6 7 8 9 10 Balanced

Finish: Short   Short-Medium   Medium   Medium-Long   Long

Tasting Experience: Poor 1 2 3 4 5 6 7 8 9 10 Excellent

Price-to-Value Ratio: Poor 1 2 3 4 5 6 7 8 9 10 Excellent

Smell

☐ TOAST	☐ COFFEE	☐ CITRUS	☐ HONEY
☐ TOBACCO	☐ SMOKE	☐ MELON	☐ APPLES
☐ LEATHER	☐ PEPPER	☐ OAK	☐ TROPICAL FRUITS
☐ MUSHROOM	☐ MINT	☐ BERRIES	☐ GRASS
☐ JAM	☐ SPICE	☐ NUTMEG	☐ FLORAL
☐ CHOCOLATE	☐ ALMOND	☐ VEGETAL	☐ _____

Taste

☐ DARK FRUITS	☐ EARTH	☐ TOAST	☐ NUTMEG
☐ BERRIES	☐ PEPPER	☐ GRASS	☐ VEGETAL
☐ PLUMS	☐ VANILLA	☐ CITRUS	☐ FLORAL
☐ MUSHROOM	☐ COFFEE	☐ MELON	☐ HONEY
☐ TOBACCO	☐ LICORICE	☐ LYCHEE	☐ PEARS
☐ CHOCOLATE	☐ LEATHER	☐ ALMOND	☐ PEACHES

WINE: _____ Vintage: _____ Producer: _____

Region/Country: _____ Price: _____ Date Tasted: _____

Grape(s): _____

Importer/Distributor: _____ Alcohol % _____

Circle Your Ratings Below

Color/Style: Red   White   Rose   Sparkling   Effervescent   Fortified
Appearance: Thin   Translucent   Saturated   Opaque
Dry/Sweet Spectrum: Dry 1 2 3 4 5 6 7 8 9 10 Sweet
Body: Light   Light-Medium   Medium   Medium-Full   Full
Balance: Unbalanced 1 2 3 4 5 6 7 8 9 10 Balanced
Finish: Short   Short-Medium   Medium   Medium-Long   Long
Tasting Experience: Poor 1 2 3 4 5 6 7 8 9 10 Excellent
Price-to-Value Ratio: Poor 1 2 3 4 5 6 7 8 9 10 Excellent

Smell

☐ TOAST	☐ COFFEE	☐ CITRUS	☐ HONEY
☐ TOBACCO	☐ SMOKE	☐ MELON	☐ APPLES
☐ LEATHER	☐ PEPPER	☐ OAK	☐ TROPICAL FRUITS
☐ MUSHROOM	☐ MINT	☐ BERRIES	☐ GRASS
☐ JAM	☐ SPICE	☐ NUTMEG	☐ FLORAL
☐ CHOCOLATE	☐ ALMOND	☐ VEGETAL	☐ _____

Taste

☐ DARK FRUITS	☐ EARTH	☐ TOAST	☐ NUTMEG
☐ BERRIES	☐ PEPPER	☐ GRASS	☐ VEGETAL
☐ PLUMS	☐ VANILLA	☐ CITRUS	☐ FLORAL
☐ MUSHROOM	☐ COFFEE	☐ MELON	☐ HONEY
☐ TOBACCO	☐ LICORICE	☐ LYCHEE	☐ PEARS
☐ CHOCOLATE	☐ LEATHER	☐ ALMOND	☐ PEACHES

WINE: _____ Vintage: _____ Producer: _____

Region/Country: _____ Price: _____ Date Tasted: _____

Grape(s): _____

Importer/Distributor: _____ Alcohol % _____

Circle Your Ratings Below

Color/Style: Red   White   Rose   Sparkling   Effervescent   Fortified
Appearance: Thin   Translucent   Saturated   Opaque
Dry/Sweet Spectrum: Dry 1 2 3 4 5 6 7 8 9 10 Sweet
Body: Light   Light-Medium   Medium   Medium-Full   Full
Balance: Unbalanced 1 2 3 4 5 6 7 8 9 10 Balanced
Finish: Short   Short-Medium   Medium   Medium-Long   Long
Tasting Experience: Poor 1 2 3 4 5 6 7 8 9 10 Excellent
Price-to-Value Ratio: Poor 1 2 3 4 5 6 7 8 9 10 Excellent

Smell

☐ TOAST	☐ COFFEE	☐ CITRUS	☐ HONEY
☐ TOBACCO	☐ SMOKE	☐ MELON	☐ APPLES
☐ LEATHER	☐ PEPPER	☐ OAK	☐ TROPICAL FRUITS
☐ MUSHROOM	☐ MINT	☐ BERRIES	☐ GRASS
☐ JAM	☐ SPICE	☐ NUTMEG	☐ FLORAL
☐ CHOCOLATE	☐ ALMOND	☐ VEGETAL	☐ _____

Taste

☐ DARK FRUITS	☐ EARTH	☐ TOAST	☐ NUTMEG
☐ BERRIES	☐ PEPPER	☐ GRASS	☐ VEGETAL
☐ PLUMS	☐ VANILLA	☐ CITRUS	☐ FLORAL
☐ MUSHROOM	☐ COFFEE	☐ MELON	☐ HONEY
☐ TOBACCO	☐ LICORICE	☐ LYCHEE	☐ PEARS
☐ CHOCOLATE	☐ LEATHER	☐ ALMOND	☐ PEACHES

WINE: _____ Vintage: _____ Producer: _____

Region/Country: _____ Price: _____ Date Tasted: _____

Grape(s): _____

Importer/Distributor: _____ Alcohol % _____

Circle Your Ratings Below

Color/Style: Red White Rose Sparkling Effervescent Fortified
Appearance: Thin Translucent Saturated Opaque
Dry/Sweet Spectrum: Dry 1 2 3 4 5 6 7 8 9 10 Sweet
Body: Light Light-Medium Medium Medium-Full Full
Balance: Unbalanced 1 2 3 4 5 6 7 8 9 10 Balanced
Finish: Short Short-Medium Medium Medium-Long Long
Tasting Experience: Poor 1 2 3 4 5 6 7 8 9 10 Excellent
Price-to-Value Ratio: Poor 1 2 3 4 5 6 7 8 9 10 Excellent

Smell

☐ TOAST	☐ COFFEE	☐ CITRUS	☐ HONEY
☐ TOBACCO	☐ SMOKE	☐ MELON	☐ APPLES
☐ LEATHER	☐ PEPPER	☐ OAK	☐ TROPICAL FRUITS
☐ MUSHROOM	☐ MINT	☐ BERRIES	☐ GRASS
☐ JAM	☐ SPICE	☐ NUTMEG	☐ FLORAL
☐ CHOCOLATE	☐ ALMOND	☐ VEGETAL	☐ _____

Taste

☐ DARK FRUITS	☐ EARTH	☐ TOAST	☐ NUTMEG
☐ BERRIES	☐ PEPPER	☐ GRASS	☐ VEGETAL
☐ PLUMS	☐ VANILLA	☐ CITRUS	☐ FLORAL
☐ MUSHROOM	☐ COFFEE	☐ MELON	☐ HONEY
☐ TOBACCO	☐ LICORICE	☐ LYCHEE	☐ PEARS
☐ CHOCOLATE	☐ LEATHER	☐ ALMOND	☐ PEACHES

WINE: _____ Vintage: _____ Producer: _____

Region/Country: _____ Price: _____ Date Tasted: _____

Grape(s): _____

Importer/Distributor: _____ Alcohol % _____

Circle Your Ratings Below

Color/Style: Red White Rose Sparkling Effervescent Fortified

Appearance: Thin Translucent Saturated Opaque

Dry/Sweet Spectrum: Dry 1 2 3 4 5 6 7 8 9 10 Sweet

Body: Light Light-Medium Medium Medium-Full Full

Balance: Unbalanced 1 2 3 4 5 6 7 8 9 10 Balanced

Finish: Short Short-Medium Medium Medium-Long Long

Tasting Experience: Poor 1 2 3 4 5 6 7 8 9 10 Excellent

Price-to-Value Ratio: Poor 1 2 3 4 5 6 7 8 9 10 Excellent

Smell

☐ TOAST	☐ COFFEE	☐ CITRUS	☐ HONEY
☐ TOBACCO	☐ SMOKE	☐ MELON	☐ APPLES
☐ LEATHER	☐ PEPPER	☐ OAK	☐ TROPICAL FRUITS
☐ MUSHROOM	☐ MINT	☐ BERRIES	☐ GRASS
☐ JAM	☐ SPICE	☐ NUTMEG	☐ FLORAL
☐ CHOCOLATE	☐ ALMOND	☐ VEGETAL	☐ _____

Taste

☐ DARK FRUITS	☐ EARTH	☐ TOAST	☐ NUTMEG
☐ BERRIES	☐ PEPPER	☐ GRASS	☐ VEGETAL
☐ PLUMS	☐ VANILLA	☐ CITRUS	☐ FLORAL
☐ MUSHROOM	☐ COFFEE	☐ MELON	☐ HONEY
☐ TOBACCO	☐ LICORICE	☐ LYCHEE	☐ PEARS
☐ CHOCOLATE	☐ LEATHER	☐ ALMOND	☐ PEACHES

Circle Your Ratings Below

Color/Style: Red   White   Rose   Sparkling   Effervescent   Fortified
Appearance: Thin   Translucent   Saturated   Opaque
Dry/Sweet Spectrum: Dry 1 2 3 4 5 6 7 8 9 10 Sweet
Body: Light   Light-Medium   Medium   Medium-Full   Full
Balance: Unbalanced 1 2 3 4 5 6 7 8 9 10 Balanced
Finish: Short   Short-Medium   Medium   Medium-Long   Long
Tasting Experience: Poor 1 2 3 4 5 6 7 8 9 10 Excellent
Price-to-Value Ratio: Poor 1 2 3 4 5 6 7 8 9 10 Excellent

Smell

☐ TOAST	☐ COFFEE	☐ CITRUS	☐ HONEY
☐ TOBACCO	☐ SMOKE	☐ MELON	☐ APPLES
☐ LEATHER	☐ PEPPER	☐ OAK	☐ TROPICAL FRUITS
☐ MUSHROOM	☐ MINT	☐ BERRIES	☐ GRASS
☐ JAM	☐ SPICE	☐ NUTMEG	☐ FLORAL
☐ CHOCOLATE	☐ ALMOND	☐ VEGETAL	☐ _____

Taste

☐ DARK FRUITS	☐ EARTH	☐ TOAST	☐ NUTMEG
☐ BERRIES	☐ PEPPER	☐ GRASS	☐ VEGETAL
☐ PLUMS	☐ VANILLA	☐ CITRUS	☐ FLORAL
☐ MUSHROOM	☐ COFFEE	☐ MELON	☐ HONEY
☐ TOBACCO	☐ LICORICE	☐ LYCHEE	☐ PEARS
☐ CHOCOLATE	☐ LEATHER	☐ ALMOND	☐ PEACHES

WINE: _____ Vintage: _____ Producer: _____

Region/Country: _____ Price: _____ Date Tasted: _____

Grape(s): _____

Importer/Distributor: _____ Alcohol % _____

Circle Your Ratings Below

Color/Style: Red   White   Rose   Sparkling   Effervescent   Fortified
Appearance: Thin   Translucent   Saturated   Opaque
Dry/Sweet Spectrum: Dry   1 2 3 4 5 6 7 8 9 10   Sweet
Body: Light   Light-Medium   Medium   Medium-Full   Full
Balance: Unbalanced   1 2 3 4 5 6 7 8 9 10   Balanced
Finish: Short   Short-Medium   Medium   Medium-Long   Long
Tasting Experience: Poor   1 2 3 4 5 6 7 8 9 10   Excellent
Price-to-Value Ratio: Poor   1 2 3 4 5 6 7 8 9 10   Excellent

Smell

☐ TOAST	☐ COFFEE	☐ CITRUS	☐ HONEY
☐ TOBACCO	☐ SMOKE	☐ MELON	☐ APPLES
☐ LEATHER	☐ PEPPER	☐ OAK	☐ TROPICAL FRUITS
☐ MUSHROOM	☐ MINT	☐ BERRIES	☐ GRASS
☐ JAM	☐ SPICE	☐ NUTMEG	☐ FLORAL
☐ CHOCOLATE	☐ ALMOND	☐ VEGETAL	☐ _____

Taste

☐ DARK FRUITS	☐ EARTH	☐ TOAST	☐ NUTMEG
☐ BERRIES	☐ PEPPER	☐ GRASS	☐ VEGETAL
☐ PLUMS	☐ VANILLA	☐ CITRUS	☐ FLORAL
☐ MUSHROOM	☐ COFFEE	☐ MELON	☐ HONEY
☐ TOBACCO	☐ LICORICE	☐ LYCHEE	☐ PEARS
☐ CHOCOLATE	☐ LEATHER	☐ ALMOND	☐ PEACHES

WINE: _____ Vintage: _____ Producer: _____

Region/Country: _____ Price: _____ Date Tasted: _____

Grape(s): _____

Importer/Distributor: _____ Alcohol % _____

Circle Your Ratings Below

Color/Style: Red   White   Rose   Sparkling   Effervescent   Fortified
Appearance: Thin   Translucent   Saturated   Opaque
Dry/Sweet Spectrum: Dry 1 2 3 4 5 6 7 8 9 10 Sweet
Body: Light   Light-Medium   Medium   Medium-Full   Full
Balance: Unbalanced 1 2 3 4 5 6 7 8 9 10 Balanced
Finish: Short   Short-Medium   Medium   Medium-Long   Long
Tasting Experience: Poor 1 2 3 4 5 6 7 8 9 10 Excellent
Price-to-Value Ratio: Poor 1 2 3 4 5 6 7 8 9 10 Excellent

Smell

☐ TOAST	☐ COFFEE	☐ CITRUS	☐ HONEY
☐ TOBACCO	☐ SMOKE	☐ MELON	☐ APPLES
☐ LEATHER	☐ PEPPER	☐ OAK	☐ TROPICAL FRUITS
☐ MUSHROOM	☐ MINT	☐ BERRIES	☐ GRASS
☐ JAM	☐ SPICE	☐ NUTMEG	☐ FLORAL
☐ CHOCOLATE	☐ ALMOND	☐ VEGETAL	☐ _____

Taste

☐ DARK FRUITS	☐ EARTH	☐ TOAST	☐ NUTMEG
☐ BERRIES	☐ PEPPER	☐ GRASS	☐ VEGETAL
☐ PLUMS	☐ VANILLA	☐ CITRUS	☐ FLORAL
☐ MUSHROOM	☐ COFFEE	☐ MELON	☐ HONEY
☐ TOBACCO	☐ LICORICE	☐ LYCHEE	☐ PEARS
☐ CHOCOLATE	☐ LEATHER	☐ ALMOND	☐ PEACHES

WINE: _____ Vintage: _____ Producer: _____

Region/Country: _____ Price: _____ Date Tasted: _____

Grape(s): _____

Importer/Distributor: _____ Alcohol % _____

Circle Your Ratings Below

Color/Style: Red   White   Rose   Sparkling   Effervescent   Fortified
Appearance: Thin   Translucent   Saturated   Opaque
Dry/Sweet Spectrum: Dry 1 2 3 4 5 6 7 8 9 10 Sweet
Body: Light   Light-Medium   Medium   Medium-Full   Full
Balance: Unbalanced 1 2 3 4 5 6 7 8 9 10 Balanced
Finish: Short   Short-Medium   Medium   Medium-Long   Long
Tasting Experience: Poor 1 2 3 4 5 6 7 8 9 10 Excellent
Price-to-Value Ratio: Poor 1 2 3 4 5 6 7 8 9 10 Excellent

Smell

☐ TOAST	☐ COFFEE	☐ CITRUS	☐ HONEY
☐ TOBACCO	☐ SMOKE	☐ MELON	☐ APPLES
☐ LEATHER	☐ PEPPER	☐ OAK	☐ TROPICAL FRUITS
☐ MUSHROOM	☐ MINT	☐ BERRIES	☐ GRASS
☐ JAM	☐ SPICE	☐ NUTMEG	☐ FLORAL
☐ CHOCOLATE	☐ ALMOND	☐ VEGETAL	☐ _____

Taste

☐ DARK FRUITS	☐ EARTH	☐ TOAST	☐ NUTMEG
☐ BERRIES	☐ PEPPER	☐ GRASS	☐ VEGETAL
☐ PLUMS	☐ VANILLA	☐ CITRUS	☐ FLORAL
☐ MUSHROOM	☐ COFFEE	☐ MELON	☐ HONEY
☐ TOBACCO	☐ LICORICE	☐ LYCHEE	☐ PEARS
☐ CHOCOLATE	☐ LEATHER	☐ ALMOND	☐ PEACHES

Circle Your Ratings Below

Color/Style: Red White Rose Sparkling Effervescent Fortified
Appearance: Thin Translucent Saturated Opaque
Dry/Sweet Spectrum: Dry 1 2 3 4 5 6 7 8 9 10 Sweet
Body: Light Light-Medium Medium Medium-Full Full
Balance: Unbalanced 1 2 3 4 5 6 7 8 9 10 Balanced
Finish: Short Short-Medium Medium Medium-Long Long
Tasting Experience: Poor 1 2 3 4 5 6 7 8 9 10 Excellent
Price-to-Value Ratio: Poor 1 2 3 4 5 6 7 8 9 10 Excellent

Smell

☐ TOAST	☐ COFFEE	☐ CITRUS	☐ HONEY
☐ TOBACCO	☐ SMOKE	☐ MELON	☐ APPLES
☐ LEATHER	☐ PEPPER	☐ OAK	☐ TROPICAL FRUITS
☐ MUSHROOM	☐ MINT	☐ BERRIES	☐ GRASS
☐ JAM	☐ SPICE	☐ NUTMEG	☐ FLORAL
☐ CHOCOLATE	☐ ALMOND	☐ VEGETAL	☐ _____

Taste

☐ DARK FRUITS	☐ EARTH	☐ TOAST	☐ NUTMEG
☐ BERRIES	☐ PEPPER	☐ GRASS	☐ VEGETAL
☐ PLUMS	☐ VANILLA	☐ CITRUS	☐ FLORAL
☐ MUSHROOM	☐ COFFEE	☐ MELON	☐ HONEY
☐ TOBACCO	☐ LICORICE	☐ LYCHEE	☐ PEARS
☐ CHOCOLATE	☐ LEATHER	☐ ALMOND	☐ PEACHES

WINE: .... Vintage: .... Producer: ....

Region/Country: .... Price: .... Date Tasted: ....

Grape(s): ....

Importer/Distributor: .... Alcohol % ....

Circle Your Ratings Below

Color/Style: Red   White   Rose   Sparkling   Effervescent   Fortified
Appearance: Thin   Translucent   Saturated   Opaque
Dry/Sweet Spectrum: Dry 1 2 3 4 5 6 7 8 9 10 Sweet
Body: Light   Light-Medium   Medium   Medium-Full   Full
Balance: Unbalanced 1 2 3 4 5 6 7 8 9 10 Balanced
Finish: Short   Short-Medium   Medium   Medium-Long   Long
Tasting Experience: Poor 1 2 3 4 5 6 7 8 9 10 Excellent
Price-to-Value Ratio: Poor 1 2 3 4 5 6 7 8 9 10 Excellent

Smell

☐ TOAST	☐ COFFEE	☐ CITRUS	☐ HONEY
☐ TOBACCO	☐ SMOKE	☐ MELON	☐ APPLES
☐ LEATHER	☐ PEPPER	☐ OAK	☐ TROPICAL FRUITS
☐ MUSHROOM	☐ MINT	☐ BERRIES	☐ GRASS
☐ JAM	☐ SPICE	☐ NUTMEG	☐ FLORAL
☐ CHOCOLATE	☐ ALMOND	☐ VEGETAL	☐ _____

Taste

☐ DARK FRUITS	☐ EARTH	☐ TOAST	☐ NUTMEG
☐ BERRIES	☐ PEPPER	☐ GRASS	☐ VEGETAL
☐ PLUMS	☐ VANILLA	☐ CITRUS	☐ FLORAL
☐ MUSHROOM	☐ COFFEE	☐ MELON	☐ HONEY
☐ TOBACCO	☐ LICORICE	☐ LYCHEE	☐ PEARS
☐ CHOCOLATE	☐ LEATHER	☐ ALMOND	☐ PEACHES

WINE: _____ Vintage: _____ Producer: _____

Region/Country: _____ Price: _____ Date Tasted: _____

Grape(s): _____

Importer/Distributor: _____ Alcohol % _____

Circle Your Ratings Below

Color/Style: Red   White   Rose   Sparkling   Effervescent   Fortified
Appearance: Thin   Translucent   Saturated   Opaque
Dry/Sweet Spectrum: Dry 1 2 3 4 5 6 7 8 9 10 Sweet
Body: Light   Light-Medium   Medium   Medium-Full   Full
Balance: Unbalanced 1 2 3 4 5 6 7 8 9 10 Balanced
Finish: Short   Short-Medium   Medium   Medium-Long   Long
Tasting Experience: Poor 1 2 3 4 5 6 7 8 9 10 Excellent
Price-to-Value Ratio: Poor 1 2 3 4 5 6 7 8 9 10 Excellent

Smell

☐ TOAST	☐ COFFEE	☐ CITRUS	☐ HONEY
☐ TOBACCO	☐ SMOKE	☐ MELON	☐ APPLES
☐ LEATHER	☐ PEPPER	☐ OAK	☐ TROPICAL FRUITS
☐ MUSHROOM	☐ MINT	☐ BERRIES	☐ GRASS
☐ JAM	☐ SPICE	☐ NUTMEG	☐ FLORAL
☐ CHOCOLATE	☐ ALMOND	☐ VEGETAL	☐ _____

Taste

☐ DARK FRUITS	☐ EARTH	☐ TOAST	☐ NUTMEG
☐ BERRIES	☐ PEPPER	☐ GRASS	☐ VEGETAL
☐ PLUMS	☐ VANILLA	☐ CITRUS	☐ FLORAL
☐ MUSHROOM	☐ COFFEE	☐ MELON	☐ HONEY
☐ TOBACCO	☐ LICORICE	☐ LYCHEE	☐ PEARS
☐ CHOCOLATE	☐ LEATHER	☐ ALMOND	☐ PEACHES

WINE: _____ Vintage: _____ Producer: _____

Region/Country: _____ Price: _____ Date Tasted: _____

Grape(s): _____

Importer/Distributor: _____ Alcohol % _____

Circle Your Ratings Below

Color/Style: Red   White   Rose   Sparkling   Effervescent   Fortified
Appearance: Thin   Translucent   Saturated   Opaque
Dry/Sweet Spectrum: Dry   1 2 3 4 5 6 7 8 9 10   Sweet
Body: Light   Light-Medium   Medium   Medium-Full   Full
Balance: Unbalanced   1 2 3 4 5 6 7 8 9 10   Balanced
Finish: Short   Short-Medium   Medium   Medium-Long   Long
Tasting Experience: Poor   1 2 3 4 5 6 7 8 9 10   Excellent
Price-to-Value Ratio: Poor   1 2 3 4 5 6 7 8 9 10   Excellent

Smell

☐ TOAST	☐ COFFEE	☐ CITRUS	☐ HONEY
☐ TOBACCO	☐ SMOKE	☐ MELON	☐ APPLES
☐ LEATHER	☐ PEPPER	☐ OAK	☐ TROPICAL FRUITS
☐ MUSHROOM	☐ MINT	☐ BERRIES	☐ GRASS
☐ JAM	☐ SPICE	☐ NUTMEG	☐ FLORAL
☐ CHOCOLATE	☐ ALMOND	☐ VEGETAL	☐ _____

Taste

☐ DARK FRUITS	☐ EARTH	☐ TOAST	☐ NUTMEG
☐ BERRIES	☐ PEPPER	☐ GRASS	☐ VEGETAL
☐ PLUMS	☐ VANILLA	☐ CITRUS	☐ FLORAL
☐ MUSHROOM	☐ COFFEE	☐ MELON	☐ HONEY
☐ TOBACCO	☐ LICORICE	☐ LYCHEE	☐ PEARS
☐ CHOCOLATE	☐ LEATHER	☐ ALMOND	☐ PEACHES

WINE: _____ Vintage: _____ Producer: _____

Region/Country: _____ Price: _____ Date Tasted: _____

Grape(s): _____

Importer/Distributor: _____ Alcohol % _____

Circle Your Ratings Below

Color/Style: Red White Rose Sparkling Effervescent Fortified

Appearance: Thin Translucent Saturated Opaque

Dry/Sweet Spectrum: Dry 1 2 3 4 5 6 7 8 9 10 Sweet

Body: Light Light-Medium Medium Medium-Full Full

Balance: Unbalanced 1 2 3 4 5 6 7 8 9 10 Balanced

Finish: Short Short-Medium Medium Medium-Long Long

Tasting Experience: Poor 1 2 3 4 5 6 7 8 9 10 Excellent

Price-to-Value Ratio: Poor 1 2 3 4 5 6 7 8 9 10 Excellent

Smell

☐ TOAST	☐ COFFEE	☐ CITRUS	☐ HONEY
☐ TOBACCO	☐ SMOKE	☐ MELON	☐ APPLES
☐ LEATHER	☐ PEPPER	☐ OAK	☐ TROPICAL FRUITS
☐ MUSHROOM	☐ MINT	☐ BERRIES	☐ GRASS
☐ JAM	☐ SPICE	☐ NUTMEG	☐ FLORAL
☐ CHOCOLATE	☐ ALMOND	☐ VEGETAL	☐ _____

Taste

☐ DARK FRUITS	☐ EARTH	☐ TOAST	☐ NUTMEG
☐ BERRIES	☐ PEPPER	☐ GRASS	☐ VEGETAL
☐ PLUMS	☐ VANILLA	☐ CITRUS	☐ FLORAL
☐ MUSHROOM	☐ COFFEE	☐ MELON	☐ HONEY
☐ TOBACCO	☐ LICORICE	☐ LYCHEE	☐ PEARS
☐ CHOCOLATE	☐ LEATHER	☐ ALMOND	☐ PEACHES

WINE: _____ Vintage:_____ Producer:_____

Region/Country: _____ Price: _____ Date Tasted:_____

Grape(s): _____

Importer/Distributor: _____ Alcohol % _____

Circle Your Ratings Below

Color/Style: Red White Rose Sparkling Effervescent Fortified
Appearance: Thin Translucent Saturated Opaque
Dry/Sweet Spectrum: Dry 1 2 3 4 5 6 7 8 9 10 Sweet
Body: Light Light-Medium Medium Medium-Full Full
Balance: Unbalanced 1 2 3 4 5 6 7 8 9 10 Balanced
Finish: Short Short-Medium Medium Medium-Long Long
Tasting Experience: Poor 1 2 3 4 5 6 7 8 9 10 Excellent
Price-to-Value Ratio: Poor 1 2 3 4 5 6 7 8 9 10 Excellent

Smell

☐ TOAST	☐ COFFEE	☐ CITRUS	☐ HONEY
☐ TOBACCO	☐ SMOKE	☐ MELON	☐ APPLES
☐ LEATHER	☐ PEPPER	☐ OAK	☐ TROPICAL FRUITS
☐ MUSHROOM	☐ MINT	☐ BERRIES	☐ GRASS
☐ JAM	☐ SPICE	☐ NUTMEG	☐ FLORAL
☐ CHOCOLATE	☐ ALMOND	☐ VEGETAL	☐ _____

Taste

☐ DARK FRUITS	☐ EARTH	☐ TOAST	☐ NUTMEG
☐ BERRIES	☐ PEPPER	☐ GRASS	☐ VEGETAL
☐ PLUMS	☐ VANILLA	☐ CITRUS	☐ FLORAL
☐ MUSHROOM	☐ COFFEE	☐ MELON	☐ HONEY
☐ TOBACCO	☐ LICORICE	☐ LYCHEE	☐ PEARS
☐ CHOCOLATE	☐ LEATHER	☐ ALMOND	☐ PEACHES

WINE: _____ Vintage: _____ Producer: _____

Region/Country: _____ Price: _____ Date Tasted: _____

Grape(s): _____

Importer/Distributor: _____ Alcohol % _____

Circle Your Ratings Below

Color/Style: Red White Rose Sparkling Effervescent Fortified
Appearance: Thin Translucent Saturated Opaque
Dry/Sweet Spectrum: Dry 1 2 3 4 5 6 7 8 9 10 Sweet
Body: Light Light-Medium Medium Medium-Full Full
Balance: Unbalanced 1 2 3 4 5 6 7 8 9 10 Balanced
Finish: Short Short-Medium Medium Medium-Long Long
Tasting Experience: Poor 1 2 3 4 5 6 7 8 9 10 Excellent
Price-to-Value Ratio: Poor 1 2 3 4 5 6 7 8 9 10 Excellent

Smell

☐ TOAST	☐ COFFEE	☐ CITRUS	☐ HONEY
☐ TOBACCO	☐ SMOKE	☐ MELON	☐ APPLES
☐ LEATHER	☐ PEPPER	☐ OAK	☐ TROPICAL FRUITS
☐ MUSHROOM	☐ MINT	☐ BERRIES	☐ GRASS
☐ JAM	☐ SPICE	☐ NUTMEG	☐ FLORAL
☐ CHOCOLATE	☐ ALMOND	☐ VEGETAL	☐ _____

Taste

☐ DARK FRUITS	☐ EARTH	☐ TOAST	☐ NUTMEG
☐ BERRIES	☐ PEPPER	☐ GRASS	☐ VEGETAL
☐ PLUMS	☐ VANILLA	☐ CITRUS	☐ FLORAL
☐ MUSHROOM	☐ COFFEE	☐ MELON	☐ HONEY
☐ TOBACCO	☐ LICORICE	☐ LYCHEE	☐ PEARS
☐ CHOCOLATE	☐ LEATHER	☐ ALMOND	☐ PEACHES

WINE: _____ Vintage: _____ Producer: _____

Region/Country: _____ Price: _____ Date Tasted: _____

Grape(s): _____

Importer/Distributor: _____ Alcohol % _____

Circle Your Ratings Below

Color/Style: Red   White   Rose   Sparkling   Effervescent   Fortified
Appearance: Thin   Translucent   Saturated   Opaque
Dry/Sweet Spectrum: Dry 1 2 3 4 5 6 7 8 9 10 Sweet
Body: Light   Light-Medium   Medium   Medium-Full   Full
Balance: Unbalanced 1 2 3 4 5 6 7 8 9 10 Balanced
Finish: Short   Short-Medium   Medium   Medium-Long   Long
Tasting Experience: Poor 1 2 3 4 5 6 7 8 9 10 Excellent
Price-to-Value Ratio: Poor 1 2 3 4 5 6 7 8 9 10 Excellent

Smell

☐ TOAST	☐ COFFEE	☐ CITRUS	☐ HONEY
☐ TOBACCO	☐ SMOKE	☐ MELON	☐ APPLES
☐ LEATHER	☐ PEPPER	☐ OAK	☐ TROPICAL FRUITS
☐ MUSHROOM	☐ MINT	☐ BERRIES	☐ GRASS
☐ JAM	☐ SPICE	☐ NUTMEG	☐ FLORAL
☐ CHOCOLATE	☐ ALMOND	☐ VEGETAL	☐ _____

Taste

☐ DARK FRUITS	☐ EARTH	☐ TOAST	☐ NUTMEG
☐ BERRIES	☐ PEPPER	☐ GRASS	☐ VEGETAL
☐ PLUMS	☐ VANILLA	☐ CITRUS	☐ FLORAL
☐ MUSHROOM	☐ COFFEE	☐ MELON	☐ HONEY
☐ TOBACCO	☐ LICORICE	☐ LYCHEE	☐ PEARS
☐ CHOCOLATE	☐ LEATHER	☐ ALMOND	☐ PEACHES

WINE: _____ Vintage: _____ Producer: _____

Region/Country: _____ Price: _____ Date Tasted: _____

Grape(s): _____

Importer/Distributor: _____ Alcohol % _____

Circle Your Ratings Below

Color/Style: Red White Rose Sparkling Effervescent Fortified
Appearance: Thin Translucent Saturated Opaque
Dry/Sweet Spectrum: Dry 1 2 3 4 5 6 7 8 9 10 Sweet
Body: Light Light-Medium Medium Medium-Full Full
Balance: Unbalanced 1 2 3 4 5 6 7 8 9 10 Balanced
Finish: Short Short-Medium Medium Medium-Long Long
Tasting Experience: Poor 1 2 3 4 5 6 7 8 9 10 Excellent
Price-to-Value Ratio: Poor 1 2 3 4 5 6 7 8 9 10 Excellent

Smell

☐ TOAST	☐ COFFEE	☐ CITRUS	☐ HONEY
☐ TOBACCO	☐ SMOKE	☐ MELON	☐ APPLES
☐ LEATHER	☐ PEPPER	☐ OAK	☐ TROPICAL FRUITS
☐ MUSHROOM	☐ MINT	☐ BERRIES	☐ GRASS
☐ JAM	☐ SPICE	☐ NUTMEG	☐ FLORAL
☐ CHOCOLATE	☐ ALMOND	☐ VEGETAL	☐ _____

Taste

☐ DARK FRUITS	☐ EARTH	☐ TOAST	☐ NUTMEG
☐ BERRIES	☐ PEPPER	☐ GRASS	☐ VEGETAL
☐ PLUMS	☐ VANILLA	☐ CITRUS	☐ FLORAL
☐ MUSHROOM	☐ COFFEE	☐ MELON	☐ HONEY
☐ TOBACCO	☐ LICORICE	☐ LYCHEE	☐ PEARS
☐ CHOCOLATE	☐ LEATHER	☐ ALMOND	☐ PEACHES

WINE: .... Vintage: .... Producer: ....

Region/Country: .... Price: .... Date Tasted: ....

Grape(s): ....

Importer/Distributor: .... Alcohol % ....

Circle Your Ratings Below

Color/Style: Red   White   Rose   Sparkling   Effervescent   Fortified
Appearance: Thin   Translucent   Saturated   Opaque
Dry/Sweet Spectrum: Dry   1   2   3   4   5   6   7   8   9   10   Sweet
Body: Light   Light-Medium   Medium   Medium-Full   Full
Balance: Unbalanced   1   2   3   4   5   6   7   8   9   10   Balanced
Finish: Short   Short-Medium   Medium   Medium-Long   Long
Tasting Experience: Poor   1   2   3   4   5   6   7   8   9   10   Excellent
Price-to-Value Ratio: Poor   1   2   3   4   5   6   7   8   9   10   Excellent

Smell

☐ TOAST	☐ COFFEE	☐ CITRUS	☐ HONEY
☐ TOBACCO	☐ SMOKE	☐ MELON	☐ APPLES
☐ LEATHER	☐ PEPPER	☐ OAK	☐ TROPICAL FRUITS
☐ MUSHROOM	☐ MINT	☐ BERRIES	☐ GRASS
☐ JAM	☐ SPICE	☐ NUTMEG	☐ FLORAL
☐ CHOCOLATE	☐ ALMOND	☐ VEGETAL	☐ _____

Taste

☐ DARK FRUITS	☐ EARTH	☐ TOAST	☐ NUTMEG
☐ BERRIES	☐ PEPPER	☐ GRASS	☐ VEGETAL
☐ PLUMS	☐ VANILLA	☐ CITRUS	☐ FLORAL
☐ MUSHROOM	☐ COFFEE	☐ MELON	☐ HONEY
☐ TOBACCO	☐ LICORICE	☐ LYCHEE	☐ PEARS
☐ CHOCOLATE	☐ LEATHER	☐ ALMOND	☐ PEACHES

WINE: _____ Vintage: _____ Producer: _____

Region/Country: _____ Price: _____ Date Tasted: _____

Grape(s): _____

Importer/Distributor: _____ Alcohol % _____

Circle Your Ratings Below

Color/Style: Red White Rose Sparkling Effervescent Fortified

Appearance: Thin Translucent Saturated Opaque

Dry/Sweet Spectrum: Dry 1 2 3 4 5 6 7 8 9 10 Sweet

Body: Light Light-Medium Medium Medium-Full Full

Balance: Unbalanced 1 2 3 4 5 6 7 8 9 10 Balanced

Finish: Short Short-Medium Medium Medium-Long Long

Tasting Experience: Poor 1 2 3 4 5 6 7 8 9 10 Excellent

Price-to-Value Ratio: Poor 1 2 3 4 5 6 7 8 9 10 Excellent

Smell

☐ TOAST	☐ COFFEE	☐ CITRUS	☐ HONEY
☐ TOBACCO	☐ SMOKE	☐ MELON	☐ APPLES
☐ LEATHER	☐ PEPPER	☐ OAK	☐ TROPICAL FRUITS
☐ MUSHROOM	☐ MINT	☐ BERRIES	☐ GRASS
☐ JAM	☐ SPICE	☐ NUTMEG	☐ FLORAL
☐ CHOCOLATE	☐ ALMOND	☐ VEGETAL	☐ _____

Taste

☐ DARK FRUITS	☐ EARTH	☐ TOAST	☐ NUTMEG
☐ BERRIES	☐ PEPPER	☐ GRASS	☐ VEGETAL
☐ PLUMS	☐ VANILLA	☐ CITRUS	☐ FLORAL
☐ MUSHROOM	☐ COFFEE	☐ MELON	☐ HONEY
☐ TOBACCO	☐ LICORICE	☐ LYCHEE	☐ PEARS
☐ CHOCOLATE	☐ LEATHER	☐ ALMOND	☐ PEACHES

WINE: _____ Vintage: _____ Producer: _____

Region/Country: _____ Price: _____ Date Tasted: _____

Grape(s): _____

Importer/Distributor: _____ Alcohol % _____

Circle Your Ratings Below

Color/Style: Red White Rose Sparkling Effervescent Fortified
Appearance: Thin Translucent Saturated Opaque
Dry/Sweet Spectrum: Dry 1 2 3 4 5 6 7 8 9 10 Sweet
Body: Light Light-Medium Medium Medium-Full Full
Balance: Unbalanced 1 2 3 4 5 6 7 8 9 10 Balanced
Finish: Short Short-Medium Medium Medium-Long Long
Tasting Experience: Poor 1 2 3 4 5 6 7 8 9 10 Excellent
Price-to-Value Ratio: Poor 1 2 3 4 5 6 7 8 9 10 Excellent

Smell

☐ TOAST	☐ COFFEE	☐ CITRUS	☐ HONEY
☐ TOBACCO	☐ SMOKE	☐ MELON	☐ APPLES
☐ LEATHER	☐ PEPPER	☐ OAK	☐ TROPICAL FRUITS
☐ MUSHROOM	☐ MINT	☐ BERRIES	☐ GRASS
☐ JAM	☐ SPICE	☐ NUTMEG	☐ FLORAL
☐ CHOCOLATE	☐ ALMOND	☐ VEGETAL	☐ _____

Taste

☐ DARK FRUITS	☐ EARTH	☐ TOAST	☐ NUTMEG
☐ BERRIES	☐ PEPPER	☐ GRASS	☐ VEGETAL
☐ PLUMS	☐ VANILLA	☐ CITRUS	☐ FLORAL
☐ MUSHROOM	☐ COFFEE	☐ MELON	☐ HONEY
☐ TOBACCO	☐ LICORICE	☐ LYCHEE	☐ PEARS
☐ CHOCOLATE	☐ LEATHER	☐ ALMOND	☐ PEACHES

WINE: _____ Vintage: _____ Producer: _____

Region/Country: _____ Price: _____ Date Tasted: _____

Grape(s): _____

Importer/Distributor: _____ Alcohol % _____

Circle Your Ratings Below

Color/Style: Red   White   Rose   Sparkling   Effervescent   Fortified
Appearance: Thin   Translucent   Saturated   Opaque
Dry/Sweet Spectrum: Dry   1 2 3 4 5 6 7 8 9 10   Sweet
Body: Light   Light-Medium   Medium   Medium-Full   Full
Balance: Unbalanced   1 2 3 4 5 6 7 8 9 10   Balanced
Finish: Short   Short-Medium   Medium   Medium-Long   Long
Tasting Experience: Poor   1 2 3 4 5 6 7 8 9 10   Excellent
Price-to-Value Ratio: Poor   1 2 3 4 5 6 7 8 9 10   Excellent

Smell

☐ TOAST	☐ COFFEE	☐ CITRUS	☐ HONEY
☐ TOBACCO	☐ SMOKE	☐ MELON	☐ APPLES
☐ LEATHER	☐ PEPPER	☐ OAK	☐ TROPICAL FRUITS
☐ MUSHROOM	☐ MINT	☐ BERRIES	☐ GRASS
☐ JAM	☐ SPICE	☐ NUTMEG	☐ FLORAL
☐ CHOCOLATE	☐ ALMOND	☐ VEGETAL	☐ _____

Taste

☐ DARK FRUITS	☐ EARTH	☐ TOAST	☐ NUTMEG
☐ BERRIES	☐ PEPPER	☐ GRASS	☐ VEGETAL
☐ PLUMS	☐ VANILLA	☐ CITRUS	☐ FLORAL
☐ MUSHROOM	☐ COFFEE	☐ MELON	☐ HONEY
☐ TOBACCO	☐ LICORICE	☐ LYCHEE	☐ PEARS
☐ CHOCOLATE	☐ LEATHER	☐ ALMOND	☐ PEACHES

WINE: .... Vintage: .... Producer: ....

Region/Country: .... Price: .... Date Tasted: ....

Grape(s): ....

Importer/Distributor: .... Alcohol % ....

Circle Your Ratings Below

Color/Style: Red   White   Rose   Sparkling   Effervescent   Fortified
Appearance: Thin   Translucent   Saturated   Opaque
Dry/Sweet Spectrum: Dry 1 2 3 4 5 6 7 8 9 10 Sweet
Body: Light   Light-Medium   Medium   Medium-Full   Full
Balance: Unbalanced 1 2 3 4 5 6 7 8 9 10 Balanced
Finish: Short   Short-Medium   Medium   Medium-Long   Long
Tasting Experience: Poor 1 2 3 4 5 6 7 8 9 10 Excellent
Price-to-Value Ratio: Poor 1 2 3 4 5 6 7 8 9 10 Excellent

Smell

☐ TOAST	☐ COFFEE	☐ CITRUS	☐ HONEY
☐ TOBACCO	☐ SMOKE	☐ MELON	☐ APPLES
☐ LEATHER	☐ PEPPER	☐ OAK	☐ TROPICAL FRUITS
☐ MUSHROOM	☐ MINT	☐ BERRIES	☐ GRASS
☐ JAM	☐ SPICE	☐ NUTMEG	☐ FLORAL
☐ CHOCOLATE	☐ ALMOND	☐ VEGETAL	☐ _____

Taste

☐ DARK FRUITS	☐ EARTH	☐ TOAST	☐ NUTMEG
☐ BERRIES	☐ PEPPER	☐ GRASS	☐ VEGETAL
☐ PLUMS	☐ VANILLA	☐ CITRUS	☐ FLORAL
☐ MUSHROOM	☐ COFFEE	☐ MELON	☐ HONEY
☐ TOBACCO	☐ LICORICE	☐ LYCHEE	☐ PEARS
☐ CHOCOLATE	☐ LEATHER	☐ ALMOND	☐ PEACHES

WINE: _____ Vintage: _____ Producer: _____

Region/Country: _____ Price: _____ Date Tasted: _____

Grape(s): _____

Importer/Distributor: _____ Alcohol % _____

Circle Your Ratings Below

Color/Style: Red White Rose Sparkling Effervescent Fortified
Appearance: Thin Translucent Saturated Opaque
Dry/Sweet Spectrum: Dry 1 2 3 4 5 6 7 8 9 10 Sweet
Body: Light Light-Medium Medium Medium-Full Full
Balance: Unbalanced 1 2 3 4 5 6 7 8 9 10 Balanced
Finish: Short Short-Medium Medium Medium-Long Long
Tasting Experience: Poor 1 2 3 4 5 6 7 8 9 10 Excellent
Price-to-Value Ratio: Poor 1 2 3 4 5 6 7 8 9 10 Excellent

Smell

☐ TOAST	☐ COFFEE	☐ CITRUS	☐ HONEY
☐ TOBACCO	☐ SMOKE	☐ MELON	☐ APPLES
☐ LEATHER	☐ PEPPER	☐ OAK	☐ TROPICAL FRUITS
☐ MUSHROOM	☐ MINT	☐ BERRIES	☐ GRASS
☐ JAM	☐ SPICE	☐ NUTMEG	☐ FLORAL
☐ CHOCOLATE	☐ ALMOND	☐ VEGETAL	☐ _____

Taste

☐ DARK FRUITS	☐ EARTH	☐ TOAST	☐ NUTMEG
☐ BERRIES	☐ PEPPER	☐ GRASS	☐ VEGETAL
☐ PLUMS	☐ VANILLA	☐ CITRUS	☐ FLORAL
☐ MUSHROOM	☐ COFFEE	☐ MELON	☐ HONEY
☐ TOBACCO	☐ LICORICE	☐ LYCHEE	☐ PEARS
☐ CHOCOLATE	☐ LEATHER	☐ ALMOND	☐ PEACHES

WINE: _____ Vintage: _____ Producer: _____

Region/Country: _____ Price: _____ Date Tasted: _____

Grape(s): _____

Importer/Distributor: _____ Alcohol % _____

Circle Your Ratings Below

Color/Style: Red White Rose Sparkling Effervescent Fortified

Appearance: Thin Translucent Saturated Opaque

Dry/Sweet Spectrum: Dry 1 2 3 4 5 6 7 8 9 10 Sweet

Body: Light Light-Medium Medium Medium-Full Full

Balance: Unbalanced 1 2 3 4 5 6 7 8 9 10 Balanced

Finish: Short Short-Medium Medium Medium-Long Long

Tasting Experience: Poor 1 2 3 4 5 6 7 8 9 10 Excellent

Price-to-Value Ratio: Poor 1 2 3 4 5 6 7 8 9 10 Excellent

Smell

☐ TOAST	☐ COFFEE	☐ CITRUS	☐ HONEY
☐ TOBACCO	☐ SMOKE	☐ MELON	☐ APPLES
☐ LEATHER	☐ PEPPER	☐ OAK	☐ TROPICAL FRUITS
☐ MUSHROOM	☐ MINT	☐ BERRIES	☐ GRASS
☐ JAM	☐ SPICE	☐ NUTMEG	☐ FLORAL
☐ CHOCOLATE	☐ ALMOND	☐ VEGETAL	☐ _____

Taste

☐ DARK FRUITS	☐ EARTH	☐ TOAST	☐ NUTMEG
☐ BERRIES	☐ PEPPER	☐ GRASS	☐ VEGETAL
☐ PLUMS	☐ VANILLA	☐ CITRUS	☐ FLORAL
☐ MUSHROOM	☐ COFFEE	☐ MELON	☐ HONEY
☐ TOBACCO	☐ LICORICE	☐ LYCHEE	☐ PEARS
☐ CHOCOLATE	☐ LEATHER	☐ ALMOND	☐ PEACHES

Circle Your Ratings Below

Color/Style: Red   White   Rose   Sparkling   Effervescent   Fortified

Appearance: Thin   Translucent   Saturated   Opaque

Dry/Sweet Spectrum: Dry   1 2 3 4 5 6 7 8 9 10   Sweet

Body: Light   Light-Medium   Medium   Medium-Full   Full

Balance: Unbalanced   1 2 3 4 5 6 7 8 9 10   Balanced

Finish: Short   Short-Medium   Medium   Medium-Long   Long

Tasting Experience: Poor   1 2 3 4 5 6 7 8 9 10   Excellent

Price-to-Value Ratio: Poor   1 2 3 4 5 6 7 8 9 10   Excellent

Smell

☐ TOAST	☐ COFFEE	☐ CITRUS	☐ HONEY
☐ TOBACCO	☐ SMOKE	☐ MELON	☐ APPLES
☐ LEATHER	☐ PEPPER	☐ OAK	☐ TROPICAL FRUITS
☐ MUSHROOM	☐ MINT	☐ BERRIES	☐ GRASS
☐ JAM	☐ SPICE	☐ NUTMEG	☐ FLORAL
☐ CHOCOLATE	☐ ALMOND	☐ VEGETAL	☐ _____

Taste

☐ DARK FRUITS	☐ EARTH	☐ TOAST	☐ NUTMEG
☐ BERRIES	☐ PEPPER	☐ GRASS	☐ VEGETAL
☐ PLUMS	☐ VANILLA	☐ CITRUS	☐ FLORAL
☐ MUSHROOM	☐ COFFEE	☐ MELON	☐ HONEY
☐ TOBACCO	☐ LICORICE	☐ LYCHEE	☐ PEARS
☐ CHOCOLATE	☐ LEATHER	☐ ALMOND	☐ PEACHES

WINE: _____ Vintage:_____ Producer:_____

Region/Country: _____ Price: _____ Date Tasted:_____

Grape(s): _____

Importer/Distributor: _____ Alcohol % _____

Circle Your Ratings Below

Color/Style: Red   White   Rose   Sparkling   Effervescent   Fortified
Appearance: Thin   Translucent   Saturated   Opaque
Dry/Sweet Spectrum: Dry 1 2 3 4 5 6 7 8 9 10 Sweet
Body: Light   Light-Medium   Medium   Medium-Full   Full
Balance: Unbalanced 1 2 3 4 5 6 7 8 9 10 Balanced
Finish: Short   Short-Medium   Medium   Medium-Long   Long
Tasting Experience: Poor 1 2 3 4 5 6 7 8 9 10 Excellent
Price-to-Value Ratio: Poor 1 2 3 4 5 6 7 8 9 10 Excellent

Smell

☐ TOAST	☐ COFFEE	☐ CITRUS	☐ HONEY
☐ TOBACCO	☐ SMOKE	☐ MELON	☐ APPLES
☐ LEATHER	☐ PEPPER	☐ OAK	☐ TROPICAL FRUITS
☐ MUSHROOM	☐ MINT	☐ BERRIES	☐ GRASS
☐ JAM	☐ SPICE	☐ NUTMEG	☐ FLORAL
☐ CHOCOLATE	☐ ALMOND	☐ VEGETAL	☐ _____

Taste

☐ DARK FRUITS	☐ EARTH	☐ TOAST	☐ NUTMEG
☐ BERRIES	☐ PEPPER	☐ GRASS	☐ VEGETAL
☐ PLUMS	☐ VANILLA	☐ CITRUS	☐ FLORAL
☐ MUSHROOM	☐ COFFEE	☐ MELON	☐ HONEY
☐ TOBACCO	☐ LICORICE	☐ LYCHEE	☐ PEARS
☐ CHOCOLATE	☐ LEATHER	☐ ALMOND	☐ PEACHES

WINE: _____ Vintage: _____ Producer: _____

Region/Country: _____ Price: _____ Date Tasted: _____

Grape(s): _____

Importer/Distributor: _____ Alcohol % _____

Circle Your Ratings Below

Color/Style: Red White Rose Sparkling Effervescent Fortified
Appearance: Thin Translucent Saturated Opaque
Dry/Sweet Spectrum: Dry 1 2 3 4 5 6 7 8 9 10 Sweet
Body: Light Light-Medium Medium Medium-Full Full
Balance: Unbalanced 1 2 3 4 5 6 7 8 9 10 Balanced
Finish: Short Short-Medium Medium Medium-Long Long
Tasting Experience: Poor 1 2 3 4 5 6 7 8 9 10 Excellent
Price-to-Value Ratio: Poor 1 2 3 4 5 6 7 8 9 10 Excellent

Smell

☐ TOAST	☐ COFFEE	☐ CITRUS	☐ HONEY
☐ TOBACCO	☐ SMOKE	☐ MELON	☐ APPLES
☐ LEATHER	☐ PEPPER	☐ OAK	☐ TROPICAL FRUITS
☐ MUSHROOM	☐ MINT	☐ BERRIES	☐ GRASS
☐ JAM	☐ SPICE	☐ NUTMEG	☐ FLORAL
☐ CHOCOLATE	☐ ALMOND	☐ VEGETAL	☐ _____

Taste

☐ DARK FRUITS	☐ EARTH	☐ TOAST	☐ NUTMEG
☐ BERRIES	☐ PEPPER	☐ GRASS	☐ VEGETAL
☐ PLUMS	☐ VANILLA	☐ CITRUS	☐ FLORAL
☐ MUSHROOM	☐ COFFEE	☐ MELON	☐ HONEY
☐ TOBACCO	☐ LICORICE	☐ LYCHEE	☐ PEARS
☐ CHOCOLATE	☐ LEATHER	☐ ALMOND	☐ PEACHES

WINE: _____ Vintage: _____ Producer: _____

Region/Country: _____ Price: _____ Date Tasted: _____

Grape(s): _____

Importer/Distributor: _____ Alcohol % _____

Circle Your Ratings Below

Color/Style: Red   White   Rose   Sparkling   Effervescent   Fortified
Appearance: Thin   Translucent   Saturated   Opaque
Dry/Sweet Spectrum: Dry   1   2   3   4   5   6   7   8   9   10   Sweet
Body: Light   Light-Medium   Medium   Medium-Full   Full
Balance: Unbalanced   1   2   3   4   5   6   7   8   9   10   Balanced
Finish: Short   Short-Medium   Medium   Medium-Long   Long
Tasting Experience: Poor   1   2   3   4   5   6   7   8   9   10   Excellent
Price-to-Value Ratio: Poor   1   2   3   4   5   6   7   8   9   10   Excellent

Smell

☐ TOAST	☐ COFFEE	☐ CITRUS	☐ HONEY
☐ TOBACCO	☐ SMOKE	☐ MELON	☐ APPLES
☐ LEATHER	☐ PEPPER	☐ OAK	☐ TROPICAL FRUITS
☐ MUSHROOM	☐ MINT	☐ BERRIES	☐ GRASS
☐ JAM	☐ SPICE	☐ NUTMEG	☐ FLORAL
☐ CHOCOLATE	☐ ALMOND	☐ VEGETAL	☐ _____

Taste

☐ DARK FRUITS	☐ EARTH	☐ TOAST	☐ NUTMEG
☐ BERRIES	☐ PEPPER	☐ GRASS	☐ VEGETAL
☐ PLUMS	☐ VANILLA	☐ CITRUS	☐ FLORAL
☐ MUSHROOM	☐ COFFEE	☐ MELON	☐ HONEY
☐ TOBACCO	☐ LICORICE	☐ LYCHEE	☐ PEARS
☐ CHOCOLATE	☐ LEATHER	☐ ALMOND	☐ PEACHES

WINE: _____ Vintage: _____ Producer: _____

Region/Country: _____ Price: _____ Date Tasted: _____

Grape(s): _____

Importer/Distributor: _____ Alcohol % _____

Circle Your Ratings Below

Color/Style: Red   White   Rose   Sparkling   Effervescent   Fortified
Appearance: Thin   Translucent   Saturated   Opaque
Dry/Sweet Spectrum: Dry   1 2 3 4 5 6 7 8 9 10   Sweet
Body: Light   Light-Medium   Medium   Medium-Full   Full
Balance: Unbalanced   1 2 3 4 5 6 7 8 9 10   Balanced
Finish: Short   Short-Medium   Medium   Medium-Long   Long
Tasting Experience: Poor   1 2 3 4 5 6 7 8 9 10   Excellent
Price-to-Value Ratio: Poor   1 2 3 4 5 6 7 8 9 10   Excellent

Smell

☐ TOAST	☐ COFFEE	☐ CITRUS	☐ HONEY
☐ TOBACCO	☐ SMOKE	☐ MELON	☐ APPLES
☐ LEATHER	☐ PEPPER	☐ OAK	☐ TROPICAL FRUITS
☐ MUSHROOM	☐ MINT	☐ BERRIES	☐ GRASS
☐ JAM	☐ SPICE	☐ NUTMEG	☐ FLORAL
☐ CHOCOLATE	☐ ALMOND	☐ VEGETAL	☐ _____

Taste

☐ DARK FRUITS	☐ EARTH	☐ TOAST	☐ NUTMEG
☐ BERRIES	☐ PEPPER	☐ GRASS	☐ VEGETAL
☐ PLUMS	☐ VANILLA	☐ CITRUS	☐ FLORAL
☐ MUSHROOM	☐ COFFEE	☐ MELON	☐ HONEY
☐ TOBACCO	☐ LICORICE	☐ LYCHEE	☐ PEARS
☐ CHOCOLATE	☐ LEATHER	☐ ALMOND	☐ PEACHES

WINE: _____ Vintage: _____ Producer: _____

Region/Country: _____ Price: _____ Date Tasted: _____

Grape(s): _____

Importer/Distributor: _____ Alcohol % _____

Circle Your Ratings Below

Color/Style: Red   White   Rose   Sparkling   Effervescent   Fortified

Appearance: Thin   Translucent   Saturated   Opaque

Dry/Sweet Spectrum: Dry 1 2 3 4 5 6 7 8 9 10 Sweet

Body: Light   Light-Medium   Medium   Medium-Full   Full

Balance: Unbalanced 1 2 3 4 5 6 7 8 9 10 Balanced

Finish: Short   Short-Medium   Medium   Medium-Long   Long

Tasting Experience: Poor   1 2 3 4 5 6 7 8 9 10 Excellent

Price-to-Value Ratio: Poor   1 2 3 4 5 6 7 8 9 10 Excellent

Smell

☐ TOAST	☐ COFFEE	☐ CITRUS	☐ HONEY
☐ TOBACCO	☐ SMOKE	☐ MELON	☐ APPLES
☐ LEATHER	☐ PEPPER	☐ OAK	☐ TROPICAL FRUITS
☐ MUSHROOM	☐ MINT	☐ BERRIES	☐ GRASS
☐ JAM	☐ SPICE	☐ NUTMEG	☐ FLORAL
☐ CHOCOLATE	☐ ALMOND	☐ VEGETAL	☐ _____

Taste

☐ DARK FRUITS	☐ EARTH	☐ TOAST	☐ NUTMEG
☐ BERRIES	☐ PEPPER	☐ GRASS	☐ VEGETAL
☐ PLUMS	☐ VANILLA	☐ CITRUS	☐ FLORAL
☐ MUSHROOM	☐ COFFEE	☐ MELON	☐ HONEY
☐ TOBACCO	☐ LICORICE	☐ LYCHEE	☐ PEARS
☐ CHOCOLATE	☐ LEATHER	☐ ALMOND	☐ PEACHES

WINE: _____ Vintage: _____ Producer: _____

Region/Country: _____ Price: _____ Date Tasted: _____

Grape(s): _____

Importer/Distributor: _____ Alcohol % _____

Circle Your Ratings Below

Color/Style: Red   White   Rose   Sparkling   Effervescent   Fortified
Appearance: Thin   Translucent   Saturated   Opaque
Dry/Sweet Spectrum: Dry   1 2 3 4 5 6 7 8 9 10   Sweet
Body: Light   Light-Medium   Medium   Medium-Full   Full
Balance: Unbalanced   1 2 3 4 5 6 7 8 9 10   Balanced
Finish: Short   Short-Medium   Medium   Medium-Long   Long
Tasting Experience: Poor   1 2 3 4 5 6 7 8 9 10   Excellent
Price-to-Value Ratio: Poor   1 2 3 4 5 6 7 8 9 10   Excellent

Smell

☐ TOAST	☐ COFFEE	☐ CITRUS	☐ HONEY
☐ TOBACCO	☐ SMOKE	☐ MELON	☐ APPLES
☐ LEATHER	☐ PEPPER	☐ OAK	☐ TROPICAL FRUITS
☐ MUSHROOM	☐ MINT	☐ BERRIES	☐ GRASS
☐ JAM	☐ SPICE	☐ NUTMEG	☐ FLORAL
☐ CHOCOLATE	☐ ALMOND	☐ VEGETAL	☐ _____

Taste

☐ DARK FRUITS	☐ EARTH	☐ TOAST	☐ NUTMEG
☐ BERRIES	☐ PEPPER	☐ GRASS	☐ VEGETAL
☐ PLUMS	☐ VANILLA	☐ CITRUS	☐ FLORAL
☐ MUSHROOM	☐ COFFEE	☐ MELON	☐ HONEY
☐ TOBACCO	☐ LICORICE	☐ LYCHEE	☐ PEARS
☐ CHOCOLATE	☐ LEATHER	☐ ALMOND	☐ PEACHES

WINE: _____ Vintage: _____ Producer: _____

Region/Country: _____ Price: _____ Date Tasted: _____

Grape(s): _____

Importer/Distributor: _____ Alcohol % _____

Circle Your Ratings Below

Color/Style: Red White Rose Sparkling Effervescent Fortified
Appearance: Thin Translucent Saturated Opaque
Dry/Sweet Spectrum: Dry 1 2 3 4 5 6 7 8 9 10 Sweet
Body: Light Light-Medium Medium Medium-Full Full
Balance: Unbalanced 1 2 3 4 5 6 7 8 9 10 Balanced
Finish: Short Short-Medium Medium Medium-Long Long
Tasting Experience: Poor 1 2 3 4 5 6 7 8 9 10 Excellent
Price-to-Value Ratio: Poor 1 2 3 4 5 6 7 8 9 10 Excellent

Smell

☐ TOAST	☐ COFFEE	☐ CITRUS	☐ HONEY
☐ TOBACCO	☐ SMOKE	☐ MELON	☐ APPLES
☐ LEATHER	☐ PEPPER	☐ OAK	☐ TROPICAL FRUITS
☐ MUSHROOM	☐ MINT	☐ BERRIES	☐ GRASS
☐ JAM	☐ SPICE	☐ NUTMEG	☐ FLORAL
☐ CHOCOLATE	☐ ALMOND	☐ VEGETAL	☐ _____

Taste

☐ DARK FRUITS	☐ EARTH	☐ TOAST	☐ NUTMEG
☐ BERRIES	☐ PEPPER	☐ GRASS	☐ VEGETAL
☐ PLUMS	☐ VANILLA	☐ CITRUS	☐ FLORAL
☐ MUSHROOM	☐ COFFEE	☐ MELON	☐ HONEY
☐ TOBACCO	☐ LICORICE	☐ LYCHEE	☐ PEARS
☐ CHOCOLATE	☐ LEATHER	☐ ALMOND	☐ PEACHES

Circle Your Ratings Below

Color/Style: Red White Rose Sparkling Effervescent Fortified

Appearance: Thin Translucent Saturated Opaque

Dry/Sweet Spectrum: Dry 1 2 3 4 5 6 7 8 9 10 Sweet

Body: Light Light-Medium Medium Medium-Full Full

Balance: Unbalanced 1 2 3 4 5 6 7 8 9 10 Balanced

Finish: Short Short-Medium Medium Medium-Long Long

Tasting Experience: Poor 1 2 3 4 5 6 7 8 9 10 Excellent

Price-to-Value Ratio: Poor 1 2 3 4 5 6 7 8 9 10 Excellent

Smell

☐ TOAST	☐ COFFEE	☐ CITRUS	☐ HONEY
☐ TOBACCO	☐ SMOKE	☐ MELON	☐ APPLES
☐ LEATHER	☐ PEPPER	☐ OAK	☐ TROPICAL FRUITS
☐ MUSHROOM	☐ MINT	☐ BERRIES	☐ GRASS
☐ JAM	☐ SPICE	☐ NUTMEG	☐ FLORAL
☐ CHOCOLATE	☐ ALMOND	☐ VEGETAL	☐ _____

Taste

☐ DARK FRUITS	☐ EARTH	☐ TOAST	☐ NUTMEG
☐ BERRIES	☐ PEPPER	☐ GRASS	☐ VEGETAL
☐ PLUMS	☐ VANILLA	☐ CITRUS	☐ FLORAL
☐ MUSHROOM	☐ COFFEE	☐ MELON	☐ HONEY
☐ TOBACCO	☐ LICORICE	☐ LYCHEE	☐ PEARS
☐ CHOCOLATE	☐ LEATHER	☐ ALMOND	☐ PEACHES

WINE: .... Vintage: .... Producer: ....

Region/Country: .... Price: .... Date Tasted: ....

Grape(s): ....

Importer/Distributor: .... Alcohol % ....

Circle Your Ratings Below

Color/Style: Red White Rose Sparkling Effervescent Fortified

Appearance: Thin Translucent Saturated Opaque

Dry/Sweet Spectrum: Dry 1 2 3 4 5 6 7 8 9 10 Sweet

Body: Light Light-Medium Medium Medium-Full Full

Balance: Unbalanced 1 2 3 4 5 6 7 8 9 10 Balanced

Finish: Short Short-Medium Medium Medium-Long Long

Tasting Experience: Poor 1 2 3 4 5 6 7 8 9 10 Excellent

Price-to-Value Ratio: Poor 1 2 3 4 5 6 7 8 9 10 Excellent

Smell

☐ TOAST	☐ COFFEE	☐ CITRUS	☐ HONEY
☐ TOBACCO	☐ SMOKE	☐ MELON	☐ APPLES
☐ LEATHER	☐ PEPPER	☐ OAK	☐ TROPICAL FRUITS
☐ MUSHROOM	☐ MINT	☐ BERRIES	☐ GRASS
☐ JAM	☐ SPICE	☐ NUTMEG	☐ FLORAL
☐ CHOCOLATE	☐ ALMOND	☐ VEGETAL	☐ _____

Taste

☐ DARK FRUITS	☐ EARTH	☐ TOAST	☐ NUTMEG
☐ BERRIES	☐ PEPPER	☐ GRASS	☐ VEGETAL
☐ PLUMS	☐ VANILLA	☐ CITRUS	☐ FLORAL
☐ MUSHROOM	☐ COFFEE	☐ MELON	☐ HONEY
☐ TOBACCO	☐ LICORICE	☐ LYCHEE	☐ PEARS
☐ CHOCOLATE	☐ LEATHER	☐ ALMOND	☐ PEACHES

WINE: _____ Vintage: _____ Producer: _____

Region/Country: _____ Price: _____ Date Tasted: _____

Grape(s): _____

Importer/Distributor: _____ Alcohol % _____

Circle Your Ratings Below

Color/Style: Red   White   Rose   Sparkling   Effervescent   Fortified

Appearance: Thin   Translucent   Saturated   Opaque

Dry/Sweet Spectrum: Dry   1 2 3 4 5 6 7 8 9 10   Sweet

Body: Light   Light-Medium   Medium   Medium-Full   Full

Balance: Unbalanced   1 2 3 4 5 6 7 8 9 10   Balanced

Finish: Short   Short-Medium   Medium   Medium-Long   Long

Tasting Experience: Poor   1 2 3 4 5 6 7 8 9 10   Excellent

Price-to-Value Ratio: Poor   1 2 3 4 5 6 7 8 9 10   Excellent

Smell

☐ TOAST	☐ COFFEE	☐ CITRUS	☐ HONEY
☐ TOBACCO	☐ SMOKE	☐ MELON	☐ APPLES
☐ LEATHER	☐ PEPPER	☐ OAK	☐ TROPICAL FRUITS
☐ MUSHROOM	☐ MINT	☐ BERRIES	☐ GRASS
☐ JAM	☐ SPICE	☐ NUTMEG	☐ FLORAL
☐ CHOCOLATE	☐ ALMOND	☐ VEGETAL	☐ _____

Taste

☐ DARK FRUITS	☐ EARTH	☐ TOAST	☐ NUTMEG
☐ BERRIES	☐ PEPPER	☐ GRASS	☐ VEGETAL
☐ PLUMS	☐ VANILLA	☐ CITRUS	☐ FLORAL
☐ MUSHROOM	☐ COFFEE	☐ MELON	☐ HONEY
☐ TOBACCO	☐ LICORICE	☐ LYCHEE	☐ PEARS
☐ CHOCOLATE	☐ LEATHER	☐ ALMOND	☐ PEACHES

WINE: _____ Vintage: _____ Producer: _____

Region/Country: _____ Price: _____ Date Tasted: _____

Grape(s): _____

Importer/Distributor: _____ Alcohol % _____

Circle Your Ratings Below

Color/Style: Red White Rose Sparkling Effervescent Fortified

Appearance: Thin Translucent Saturated Opaque

Dry/Sweet Spectrum: Dry 1 2 3 4 5 6 7 8 9 10 Sweet

Body: Light Light-Medium Medium Medium-Full Full

Balance: Unbalanced 1 2 3 4 5 6 7 8 9 10 Balanced

Finish: Short Short-Medium Medium Medium-Long Long

Tasting Experience: Poor 1 2 3 4 5 6 7 8 9 10 Excellent

Price-to-Value Ratio: Poor 1 2 3 4 5 6 7 8 9 10 Excellent

Smell

☐ TOAST	☐ COFFEE	☐ CITRUS	☐ HONEY
☐ TOBACCO	☐ SMOKE	☐ MELON	☐ APPLES
☐ LEATHER	☐ PEPPER	☐ OAK	☐ TROPICAL FRUITS
☐ MUSHROOM	☐ MINT	☐ BERRIES	☐ GRASS
☐ JAM	☐ SPICE	☐ NUTMEG	☐ FLORAL
☐ CHOCOLATE	☐ ALMOND	☐ VEGETAL	☐ _____

Taste

☐ DARK FRUITS	☐ EARTH	☐ TOAST	☐ NUTMEG
☐ BERRIES	☐ PEPPER	☐ GRASS	☐ VEGETAL
☐ PLUMS	☐ VANILLA	☐ CITRUS	☐ FLORAL
☐ MUSHROOM	☐ COFFEE	☐ MELON	☐ HONEY
☐ TOBACCO	☐ LICORICE	☐ LYCHEE	☐ PEARS
☐ CHOCOLATE	☐ LEATHER	☐ ALMOND	☐ PEACHES

Circle Your Ratings Below

Color/Style: Red White Rose Sparkling Effervescent Fortified
Appearance: Thin Translucent Saturated Opaque
Dry/Sweet Spectrum: Dry 1 2 3 4 5 6 7 8 9 10 Sweet
Body: Light Light-Medium Medium Medium-Full Full
Balance: Unbalanced 1 2 3 4 5 6 7 8 9 10 Balanced
Finish: Short Short-Medium Medium Medium-Long Long
Tasting Experience: Poor 1 2 3 4 5 6 7 8 9 10 Excellent
Price-to-Value Ratio: Poor 1 2 3 4 5 6 7 8 9 10 Excellent

Smell

☐ TOAST	☐ COFFEE	☐ CITRUS	☐ HONEY
☐ TOBACCO	☐ SMOKE	☐ MELON	☐ APPLES
☐ LEATHER	☐ PEPPER	☐ OAK	☐ TROPICAL FRUITS
☐ MUSHROOM	☐ MINT	☐ BERRIES	☐ GRASS
☐ JAM	☐ SPICE	☐ NUTMEG	☐ FLORAL
☐ CHOCOLATE	☐ ALMOND	☐ VEGETAL	☐ _____

Taste

☐ DARK FRUITS	☐ EARTH	☐ TOAST	☐ NUTMEG
☐ BERRIES	☐ PEPPER	☐ GRASS	☐ VEGETAL
☐ PLUMS	☐ VANILLA	☐ CITRUS	☐ FLORAL
☐ MUSHROOM	☐ COFFEE	☐ MELON	☐ HONEY
☐ TOBACCO	☐ LICORICE	☐ LYCHEE	☐ PEARS
☐ CHOCOLATE	☐ LEATHER	☐ ALMOND	☐ PEACHES

WINE: _____ Vintage: _____ Producer: _____

Region/Country: _____ Price: _____ Date Tasted: _____

Grape(s): _____

Importer/Distributor: _____ Alcohol % _____

Circle Your Ratings Below

Color/Style: Red White Rose Sparkling Effervescent Fortified

Appearance: Thin Translucent Saturated Opaque

Dry/Sweet Spectrum: Dry 1 2 3 4 5 6 7 8 9 10 Sweet

Body: Light Light-Medium Medium Medium-Full Full

Balance: Unbalanced 1 2 3 4 5 6 7 8 9 10 Balanced

Finish: Short Short-Medium Medium Medium-Long Long

Tasting Experience: Poor 1 2 3 4 5 6 7 8 9 10 Excellent

Price-to-Value Ratio: Poor 1 2 3 4 5 6 7 8 9 10 Excellent

Smell

☐ TOAST	☐ COFFEE	☐ CITRUS	☐ HONEY
☐ TOBACCO	☐ SMOKE	☐ MELON	☐ APPLES
☐ LEATHER	☐ PEPPER	☐ OAK	☐ TROPICAL FRUITS
☐ MUSHROOM	☐ MINT	☐ BERRIES	☐ GRASS
☐ JAM	☐ SPICE	☐ NUTMEG	☐ FLORAL
☐ CHOCOLATE	☐ ALMOND	☐ VEGETAL	☐ _____

Taste

☐ DARK FRUITS	☐ EARTH	☐ TOAST	☐ NUTMEG
☐ BERRIES	☐ PEPPER	☐ GRASS	☐ VEGETAL
☐ PLUMS	☐ VANILLA	☐ CITRUS	☐ FLORAL
☐ MUSHROOM	☐ COFFEE	☐ MELON	☐ HONEY
☐ TOBACCO	☐ LICORICE	☐ LYCHEE	☐ PEARS
☐ CHOCOLATE	☐ LEATHER	☐ ALMOND	☐ PEACHES

WINE: _____ Vintage: _____ Producer: _____

Region/Country: _____ Price: _____ Date Tasted: _____

Grape(s): _____

Importer/Distributor: _____ Alcohol % _____

Circle Your Ratings Below

Color/Style: Red   White   Rose   Sparkling   Effervescent   Fortified

Appearance: Thin   Translucent   Saturated   Opaque

Dry/Sweet Spectrum: Dry 1 2 3 4 5 6 7 8 9 10 Sweet

Body: Light   Light-Medium   Medium   Medium-Full   Full

Balance: Unbalanced 1 2 3 4 5 6 7 8 9 10 Balanced

Finish: Short   Short-Medium   Medium   Medium-Long   Long

Tasting Experience: Poor 1 2 3 4 5 6 7 8 9 10 Excellent

Price-to-Value Ratio: Poor 1 2 3 4 5 6 7 8 9 10 Excellent

Smell

☐ TOAST	☐ COFFEE	☐ CITRUS	☐ HONEY
☐ TOBACCO	☐ SMOKE	☐ MELON	☐ APPLES
☐ LEATHER	☐ PEPPER	☐ OAK	☐ TROPICAL FRUITS
☐ MUSHROOM	☐ MINT	☐ BERRIES	☐ GRASS
☐ JAM	☐ SPICE	☐ NUTMEG	☐ FLORAL
☐ CHOCOLATE	☐ ALMOND	☐ VEGETAL	☐ _____

Taste

☐ DARK FRUITS	☐ EARTH	☐ TOAST	☐ NUTMEG
☐ BERRIES	☐ PEPPER	☐ GRASS	☐ VEGETAL
☐ PLUMS	☐ VANILLA	☐ CITRUS	☐ FLORAL
☐ MUSHROOM	☐ COFFEE	☐ MELON	☐ HONEY
☐ TOBACCO	☐ LICORICE	☐ LYCHEE	☐ PEARS
☐ CHOCOLATE	☐ LEATHER	☐ ALMOND	☐ PEACHES

WINE: _____ Vintage: _____ Producer: _____

Region/Country: _____ Price: _____ Date Tasted: _____

Grape(s): _____

Importer/Distributor: _____ Alcohol % _____

Circle Your Ratings Below

Color/Style: Red White Rose Sparkling Effervescent Fortified

Appearance: Thin Translucent Saturated Opaque

Dry/Sweet Spectrum: Dry 1 2 3 4 5 6 7 8 9 10 Sweet

Body: Light Light-Medium Medium Medium-Full Full

Balance: Unbalanced 1 2 3 4 5 6 7 8 9 10 Balanced

Finish: Short Short-Medium Medium Medium-Long Long

Tasting Experience: Poor 1 2 3 4 5 6 7 8 9 10 Excellent

Price-to-Value Ratio: Poor 1 2 3 4 5 6 7 8 9 10 Excellent

Smell

☐ TOAST	☐ COFFEE	☐ CITRUS	☐ HONEY
☐ TOBACCO	☐ SMOKE	☐ MELON	☐ APPLES
☐ LEATHER	☐ PEPPER	☐ OAK	☐ TROPICAL FRUITS
☐ MUSHROOM	☐ MINT	☐ BERRIES	☐ GRASS
☐ JAM	☐ SPICE	☐ NUTMEG	☐ FLORAL
☐ CHOCOLATE	☐ ALMOND	☐ VEGETAL	☐ _____

Taste

☐ DARK FRUITS	☐ EARTH	☐ TOAST	☐ NUTMEG
☐ BERRIES	☐ PEPPER	☐ GRASS	☐ VEGETAL
☐ PLUMS	☐ VANILLA	☐ CITRUS	☐ FLORAL
☐ MUSHROOM	☐ COFFEE	☐ MELON	☐ HONEY
☐ TOBACCO	☐ LICORICE	☐ LYCHEE	☐ PEARS
☐ CHOCOLATE	☐ LEATHER	☐ ALMOND	☐ PEACHES

WINE: _____ Vintage: _____ Producer: _____

Region/Country: _____ Price: _____ Date Tasted: _____

Grape(s): _____

Importer/Distributor: _____ Alcohol % _____

Circle Your Ratings Below

Color/Style: Red White Rose Sparkling Effervescent Fortified
Appearance: Thin Translucent Saturated Opaque
Dry/Sweet Spectrum: Dry 1 2 3 4 5 6 7 8 9 10 Sweet
Body: Light Light-Medium Medium Medium-Full Full
Balance: Unbalanced 1 2 3 4 5 6 7 8 9 10 Balanced
Finish: Short Short-Medium Medium Medium-Long Long
Tasting Experience: Poor 1 2 3 4 5 6 7 8 9 10 Excellent
Price-to-Value Ratio: Poor 1 2 3 4 5 6 7 8 9 10 Excellent

Smell

☐ TOAST	☐ COFFEE	☐ CITRUS	☐ HONEY
☐ TOBACCO	☐ SMOKE	☐ MELON	☐ APPLES
☐ LEATHER	☐ PEPPER	☐ OAK	☐ TROPICAL FRUITS
☐ MUSHROOM	☐ MINT	☐ BERRIES	☐ GRASS
☐ JAM	☐ SPICE	☐ NUTMEG	☐ FLORAL
☐ CHOCOLATE	☐ ALMOND	☐ VEGETAL	☐ _____

Taste

☐ DARK FRUITS	☐ EARTH	☐ TOAST	☐ NUTMEG
☐ BERRIES	☐ PEPPER	☐ GRASS	☐ VEGETAL
☐ PLUMS	☐ VANILLA	☐ CITRUS	☐ FLORAL
☐ MUSHROOM	☐ COFFEE	☐ MELON	☐ HONEY
☐ TOBACCO	☐ LICORICE	☐ LYCHEE	☐ PEARS
☐ CHOCOLATE	☐ LEATHER	☐ ALMOND	☐ PEACHES

WINE: .... Vintage: .... Producer: ....

Region/Country: .... Price: .... Date Tasted: ....

Grape(s): ....

Importer/Distributor: .... Alcohol % ....

Circle Your Ratings Below

Color/Style: Red White Rose Sparkling Effervescent Fortified
Appearance: Thin Translucent Saturated Opaque
Dry/Sweet Spectrum: Dry 1 2 3 4 5 6 7 8 9 10 Sweet
Body: Light Light-Medium Medium Medium-Full Full
Balance: Unbalanced 1 2 3 4 5 6 7 8 9 10 Balanced
Finish: Short Short-Medium Medium Medium-Long Long
Tasting Experience: Poor 1 2 3 4 5 6 7 8 9 10 Excellent
Price-to-Value Ratio: Poor 1 2 3 4 5 6 7 8 9 10 Excellent

Smell

☐ TOAST	☐ COFFEE	☐ CITRUS	☐ HONEY
☐ TOBACCO	☐ SMOKE	☐ MELON	☐ APPLES
☐ LEATHER	☐ PEPPER	☐ OAK	☐ TROPICAL FRUITS
☐ MUSHROOM	☐ MINT	☐ BERRIES	☐ GRASS
☐ JAM	☐ SPICE	☐ NUTMEG	☐ FLORAL
☐ CHOCOLATE	☐ ALMOND	☐ VEGETAL	☐ _____

Taste

☐ DARK FRUITS	☐ EARTH	☐ TOAST	☐ NUTMEG
☐ BERRIES	☐ PEPPER	☐ GRASS	☐ VEGETAL
☐ PLUMS	☐ VANILLA	☐ CITRUS	☐ FLORAL
☐ MUSHROOM	☐ COFFEE	☐ MELON	☐ HONEY
☐ TOBACCO	☐ LICORICE	☐ LYCHEE	☐ PEARS
☐ CHOCOLATE	☐ LEATHER	☐ ALMOND	☐ PEACHES

WINE: _____ Vintage: _____ Producer: _____

Region/Country: _____ Price: _____ Date Tasted: _____

Grape(s): _____

Importer/Distributor: _____ Alcohol % _____

Circle Your Ratings Below

Color/Style: Red   White   Rose   Sparkling   Effervescent   Fortified
Appearance: Thin   Translucent   Saturated   Opaque
Dry/Sweet Spectrum: Dry   1   2   3   4   5   6   7   8   9   10   Sweet
Body: Light   Light-Medium   Medium   Medium-Full   Full
Balance: Unbalanced   1   2   3   4   5   6   7   8   9   10   Balanced
Finish: Short   Short-Medium   Medium   Medium-Long   Long
Tasting Experience: Poor   1   2   3   4   5   6   7   8   9   10   Excellent
Price-to-Value Ratio: Poor   1   2   3   4   5   6   7   8   9   10   Excellent

Smell

☐ TOAST	☐ COFFEE	☐ CITRUS	☐ HONEY
☐ TOBACCO	☐ SMOKE	☐ MELON	☐ APPLES
☐ LEATHER	☐ PEPPER	☐ OAK	☐ TROPICAL FRUITS
☐ MUSHROOM	☐ MINT	☐ BERRIES	☐ GRASS
☐ JAM	☐ SPICE	☐ NUTMEG	☐ FLORAL
☐ CHOCOLATE	☐ ALMOND	☐ VEGETAL	☐ _____

Taste

☐ DARK FRUITS	☐ EARTH	☐ TOAST	☐ NUTMEG
☐ BERRIES	☐ PEPPER	☐ GRASS	☐ VEGETAL
☐ PLUMS	☐ VANILLA	☐ CITRUS	☐ FLORAL
☐ MUSHROOM	☐ COFFEE	☐ MELON	☐ HONEY
☐ TOBACCO	☐ LICORICE	☐ LYCHEE	☐ PEARS
☐ CHOCOLATE	☐ LEATHER	☐ ALMOND	☐ PEACHES

WINE: .... Vintage: .... Producer: ....

Region/Country: .... Price: .... Date Tasted: ....

Grape(s): ....

Importer/Distributor: .... Alcohol % ....

Circle Your Ratings Below

Color/Style: Red   White   Rose   Sparkling   Effervescent   Fortified
Appearance: Thin   Translucent   Saturated   Opaque
Dry/Sweet Spectrum: Dry   1 2 3 4 5 6 7 8 9 10   Sweet
Body: Light   Light-Medium   Medium   Medium-Full   Full
Balance: Unbalanced   1 2 3 4 5 6 7 8 9 10   Balanced
Finish: Short   Short-Medium   Medium   Medium-Long   Long
Tasting Experience: Poor   1 2 3 4 5 6 7 8 9 10   Excellent
Price-to-Value Ratio: Poor   1 2 3 4 5 6 7 8 9 10   Excellent

Smell

☐ TOAST	☐ COFFEE	☐ CITRUS	☐ HONEY
☐ TOBACCO	☐ SMOKE	☐ MELON	☐ APPLES
☐ LEATHER	☐ PEPPER	☐ OAK	☐ TROPICAL FRUITS
☐ MUSHROOM	☐ MINT	☐ BERRIES	☐ GRASS
☐ JAM	☐ SPICE	☐ NUTMEG	☐ FLORAL
☐ CHOCOLATE	☐ ALMOND	☐ VEGETAL	☐ _____

Taste

☐ DARK FRUITS	☐ EARTH	☐ TOAST	☐ NUTMEG
☐ BERRIES	☐ PEPPER	☐ GRASS	☐ VEGETAL
☐ PLUMS	☐ VANILLA	☐ CITRUS	☐ FLORAL
☐ MUSHROOM	☐ COFFEE	☐ MELON	☐ HONEY
☐ TOBACCO	☐ LICORICE	☐ LYCHEE	☐ PEARS
☐ CHOCOLATE	☐ LEATHER	☐ ALMOND	☐ PEACHES

WINE: _____ Vintage: _____ Producer: _____

Region/Country: _____ Price: _____ Date Tasted: _____

Grape(s): _____

Importer/Distributor: _____ Alcohol % _____

Circle Your Ratings Below

Color/Style: Red   White   Rose   Sparkling   Effervescent   Fortified
Appearance: Thin   Translucent   Saturated   Opaque
Dry/Sweet Spectrum: Dry 1 2 3 4 5 6 7 8 9 10 Sweet
Body: Light   Light-Medium   Medium   Medium-Full   Full
Balance: Unbalanced 1 2 3 4 5 6 7 8 9 10 Balanced
Finish: Short   Short-Medium   Medium   Medium-Long   Long
Tasting Experience: Poor 1 2 3 4 5 6 7 8 9 10 Excellent
Price-to-Value Ratio: Poor 1 2 3 4 5 6 7 8 9 10 Excellent

Smell

☐ TOAST	☐ COFFEE	☐ CITRUS	☐ HONEY
☐ TOBACCO	☐ SMOKE	☐ MELON	☐ APPLES
☐ LEATHER	☐ PEPPER	☐ OAK	☐ TROPICAL FRUITS
☐ MUSHROOM	☐ MINT	☐ BERRIES	☐ GRASS
☐ JAM	☐ SPICE	☐ NUTMEG	☐ FLORAL
☐ CHOCOLATE	☐ ALMOND	☐ VEGETAL	☐ _____

Taste

☐ DARK FRUITS	☐ EARTH	☐ TOAST	☐ NUTMEG
☐ BERRIES	☐ PEPPER	☐ GRASS	☐ VEGETAL
☐ PLUMS	☐ VANILLA	☐ CITRUS	☐ FLORAL
☐ MUSHROOM	☐ COFFEE	☐ MELON	☐ HONEY
☐ TOBACCO	☐ LICORICE	☐ LYCHEE	☐ PEARS
☐ CHOCOLATE	☐ LEATHER	☐ ALMOND	☐ PEACHES

WINE: _____ Vintage: _____ Producer: _____

Region/Country: _____ Price: _____ Date Tasted: _____

Grape(s): _____

Importer/Distributor: _____ Alcohol % _____

Circle Your Ratings Below

Color/Style: Red   White   Rose   Sparkling   Effervescent   Fortified
Appearance: Thin   Translucent   Saturated   Opaque
Dry/Sweet Spectrum: Dry 1 2 3 4 5 6 7 8 9 10 Sweet
Body: Light   Light-Medium   Medium   Medium-Full   Full
Balance: Unbalanced 1 2 3 4 5 6 7 8 9 10 Balanced
Finish: Short   Short-Medium   Medium   Medium-Long   Long
Tasting Experience: Poor 1 2 3 4 5 6 7 8 9 10 Excellent
Price-to-Value Ratio: Poor 1 2 3 4 5 6 7 8 9 10 Excellent

Smell

☐ TOAST	☐ COFFEE	☐ CITRUS	☐ HONEY
☐ TOBACCO	☐ SMOKE	☐ MELON	☐ APPLES
☐ LEATHER	☐ PEPPER	☐ OAK	☐ TROPICAL FRUITS
☐ MUSHROOM	☐ MINT	☐ BERRIES	☐ GRASS
☐ JAM	☐ SPICE	☐ NUTMEG	☐ FLORAL
☐ CHOCOLATE	☐ ALMOND	☐ VEGETAL	☐ _____

Taste

☐ DARK FRUITS	☐ EARTH	☐ TOAST	☐ NUTMEG
☐ BERRIES	☐ PEPPER	☐ GRASS	☐ VEGETAL
☐ PLUMS	☐ VANILLA	☐ CITRUS	☐ FLORAL
☐ MUSHROOM	☐ COFFEE	☐ MELON	☐ HONEY
☐ TOBACCO	☐ LICORICE	☐ LYCHEE	☐ PEARS
☐ CHOCOLATE	☐ LEATHER	☐ ALMOND	☐ PEACHES

WINE: _____ Vintage: _____ Producer: _____

Region/Country: _____ Price: _____ Date Tasted: _____

Grape(s): _____

Importer/Distributor: _____ Alcohol % _____

Circle Your Ratings Below

Color/Style: Red   White   Rose   Sparkling   Effervescent   Fortified
Appearance: Thin   Translucent   Saturated   Opaque
Dry/Sweet Spectrum: Dry 1 2 3 4 5 6 7 8 9 10 Sweet
Body: Light   Light-Medium   Medium   Medium-Full   Full
Balance: Unbalanced 1 2 3 4 5 6 7 8 9 10 Balanced
Finish: Short   Short-Medium   Medium   Medium-Long   Long
Tasting Experience: Poor   1 2 3 4 5 6 7 8 9 10 Excellent
Price-to-Value Ratio: Poor   1 2 3 4 5 6 7 8 9 10 Excellent

Smell

☐ TOAST	☐ COFFEE	☐ CITRUS	☐ HONEY
☐ TOBACCO	☐ SMOKE	☐ MELON	☐ APPLES
☐ LEATHER	☐ PEPPER	☐ OAK	☐ TROPICAL FRUITS
☐ MUSHROOM	☐ MINT	☐ BERRIES	☐ GRASS
☐ JAM	☐ SPICE	☐ NUTMEG	☐ FLORAL
☐ CHOCOLATE	☐ ALMOND	☐ VEGETAL	☐ _____

Taste

☐ DARK FRUITS	☐ EARTH	☐ TOAST	☐ NUTMEG
☐ BERRIES	☐ PEPPER	☐ GRASS	☐ VEGETAL
☐ PLUMS	☐ VANILLA	☐ CITRUS	☐ FLORAL
☐ MUSHROOM	☐ COFFEE	☐ MELON	☐ HONEY
☐ TOBACCO	☐ LICORICE	☐ LYCHEE	☐ PEARS
☐ CHOCOLATE	☐ LEATHER	☐ ALMOND	☐ PEACHES

WINE: _____ Vintage: _____ Producer: _____

Region/Country: _____ Price: _____ Date Tasted: _____

Grape(s): _____

Importer/Distributor: _____ Alcohol % _____

Circle Your Ratings Below

Color/Style: Red   White   Rose   Sparkling   Effervescent   Fortified
Appearance: Thin   Translucent   Saturated   Opaque
Dry/Sweet Spectrum: Dry 1 2 3 4 5 6 7 8 9 10 Sweet
Body: Light   Light-Medium   Medium   Medium-Full   Full
Balance: Unbalanced 1 2 3 4 5 6 7 8 9 10 Balanced
Finish: Short   Short-Medium   Medium   Medium-Long   Long
Tasting Experience: Poor   1 2 3 4 5 6 7 8 9 10 Excellent
Price-to-Value Ratio: Poor   1 2 3 4 5 6 7 8 9 10 Excellent

Smell

☐ TOAST	☐ COFFEE	☐ CITRUS	☐ HONEY
☐ TOBACCO	☐ SMOKE	☐ MELON	☐ APPLES
☐ LEATHER	☐ PEPPER	☐ OAK	☐ TROPICAL FRUITS
☐ MUSHROOM	☐ MINT	☐ BERRIES	☐ GRASS
☐ JAM	☐ SPICE	☐ NUTMEG	☐ FLORAL
☐ CHOCOLATE	☐ ALMOND	☐ VEGETAL	☐ _____

Taste

☐ DARK FRUITS	☐ EARTH	☐ TOAST	☐ NUTMEG
☐ BERRIES	☐ PEPPER	☐ GRASS	☐ VEGETAL
☐ PLUMS	☐ VANILLA	☐ CITRUS	☐ FLORAL
☐ MUSHROOM	☐ COFFEE	☐ MELON	☐ HONEY
☐ TOBACCO	☐ LICORICE	☐ LYCHEE	☐ PEARS
☐ CHOCOLATE	☐ LEATHER	☐ ALMOND	☐ PEACHES

WINE: _____ Vintage:_____ Producer:_____

Region/Country: _____ Price: _____ Date Tasted: _____

Grape(s): _____

Importer/Distributor: _____ Alcohol % _____

Circle Your Ratings Below

Color/Style: Red   White   Rose   Sparkling   Effervescent   Fortified
Appearance: Thin   Translucent   Saturated   Opaque
Dry/Sweet Spectrum: Dry 1 2 3 4 5 6 7 8 9 10 Sweet
Body: Light   Light-Medium   Medium   Medium-Full   Full
Balance: Unbalanced 1 2 3 4 5 6 7 8 9 10 Balanced
Finish: Short   Short-Medium   Medium   Medium-Long   Long
Tasting Experience: Poor   1 2 3 4 5 6 7 8 9 10 Excellent
Price-to-Value Ratio: Poor   1 2 3 4 5 6 7 8 9 10 Excellent

Smell

☐ TOAST	☐ COFFEE	☐ CITRUS	☐ HONEY
☐ TOBACCO	☐ SMOKE	☐ MELON	☐ APPLES
☐ LEATHER	☐ PEPPER	☐ OAK	☐ TROPICAL FRUITS
☐ MUSHROOM	☐ MINT	☐ BERRIES	☐ GRASS
☐ JAM	☐ SPICE	☐ NUTMEG	☐ FLORAL
☐ CHOCOLATE	☐ ALMOND	☐ VEGETAL	☐ _____

Taste

☐ DARK FRUITS	☐ EARTH	☐ TOAST	☐ NUTMEG
☐ BERRIES	☐ PEPPER	☐ GRASS	☐ VEGETAL
☐ PLUMS	☐ VANILLA	☐ CITRUS	☐ FLORAL
☐ MUSHROOM	☐ COFFEE	☐ MELON	☐ HONEY
☐ TOBACCO	☐ LICORICE	☐ LYCHEE	☐ PEARS
☐ CHOCOLATE	☐ LEATHER	☐ ALMOND	☐ PEACHES

WINE: _____ Vintage: _____ Producer: _____

Region/Country: _____ Price: _____ Date Tasted: _____

Grape(s): _____

Importer/Distributor: _____ Alcohol % _____

Circle Your Ratings Below

Color/Style: Red White Rose Sparkling Effervescent Fortified

Appearance: Thin Translucent Saturated Opaque

Dry/Sweet Spectrum: Dry 1 2 3 4 5 6 7 8 9 10 Sweet

Body: Light Light-Medium Medium Medium-Full Full

Balance: Unbalanced 1 2 3 4 5 6 7 8 9 10 Balanced

Finish: Short Short-Medium Medium Medium-Long Long

Tasting Experience: Poor 1 2 3 4 5 6 7 8 9 10 Excellent

Price-to-Value Ratio: Poor 1 2 3 4 5 6 7 8 9 10 Excellent

Smell

☐ TOAST	☐ COFFEE	☐ CITRUS	☐ HONEY
☐ TOBACCO	☐ SMOKE	☐ MELON	☐ APPLES
☐ LEATHER	☐ PEPPER	☐ OAK	☐ TROPICAL FRUITS
☐ MUSHROOM	☐ MINT	☐ BERRIES	☐ GRASS
☐ JAM	☐ SPICE	☐ NUTMEG	☐ FLORAL
☐ CHOCOLATE	☐ ALMOND	☐ VEGETAL	☐ _____

Taste

☐ DARK FRUITS	☐ EARTH	☐ TOAST	☐ NUTMEG
☐ BERRIES	☐ PEPPER	☐ GRASS	☐ VEGETAL
☐ PLUMS	☐ VANILLA	☐ CITRUS	☐ FLORAL
☐ MUSHROOM	☐ COFFEE	☐ MELON	☐ HONEY
☐ TOBACCO	☐ LICORICE	☐ LYCHEE	☐ PEARS
☐ CHOCOLATE	☐ LEATHER	☐ ALMOND	☐ PEACHES

WINE: _____ Vintage:_____ Producer:_____

Region/Country: _____ Price: _____ Date Tasted:_____

Grape(s): _____

Importer/Distributor: _____ Alcohol % _____

Circle Your Ratings Below

Color/Style: Red White Rose Sparkling Effervescent Fortified
Appearance: Thin Translucent Saturated Opaque
Dry/Sweet Spectrum: Dry 1 2 3 4 5 6 7 8 9 10 Sweet
Body: Light Light-Medium Medium Medium-Full Full
Balance: Unbalanced 1 2 3 4 5 6 7 8 9 10 Balanced
Finish: Short Short-Medium Medium Medium-Long Long
Tasting Experience: Poor 1 2 3 4 5 6 7 8 9 10 Excellent
Price-to-Value Ratio: Poor 1 2 3 4 5 6 7 8 9 10 Excellent

Smell

☐ TOAST	☐ COFFEE	☐ CITRUS	☐ HONEY
☐ TOBACCO	☐ SMOKE	☐ MELON	☐ APPLES
☐ LEATHER	☐ PEPPER	☐ OAK	☐ TROPICAL FRUITS
☐ MUSHROOM	☐ MINT	☐ BERRIES	☐ GRASS
☐ JAM	☐ SPICE	☐ NUTMEG	☐ FLORAL
☐ CHOCOLATE	☐ ALMOND	☐ VEGETAL	☐ _____

Taste

☐ DARK FRUITS	☐ EARTH	☐ TOAST	☐ NUTMEG
☐ BERRIES	☐ PEPPER	☐ GRASS	☐ VEGETAL
☐ PLUMS	☐ VANILLA	☐ CITRUS	☐ FLORAL
☐ MUSHROOM	☐ COFFEE	☐ MELON	☐ HONEY
☐ TOBACCO	☐ LICORICE	☐ LYCHEE	☐ PEARS
☐ CHOCOLATE	☐ LEATHER	☐ ALMOND	☐ PEACHES

WINE: _____ Vintage: _____ Producer: _____

Region/Country: _____ Price: _____ Date Tasted: _____

Grape(s): _____

Importer/Distributor: _____ Alcohol % _____

Circle Your Ratings Below

Color/Style: Red   White   Rose   Sparkling   Effervescent   Fortified
Appearance: Thin   Translucent   Saturated   Opaque
Dry/Sweet Spectrum: Dry 1 2 3 4 5 6 7 8 9 10   Sweet
Body: Light   Light-Medium   Medium   Medium-Full   Full
Balance: Unbalanced 1 2 3 4 5 6 7 8 9 10   Balanced
Finish: Short   Short-Medium   Medium   Medium-Long   Long
Tasting Experience: Poor   1 2 3 4 5 6 7 8 9 10   Excellent
Price-to-Value Ratio: Poor   1 2 3 4 5 6 7 8 9 10   Excellent

Smell

☐ TOAST	☐ COFFEE	☐ CITRUS	☐ HONEY
☐ TOBACCO	☐ SMOKE	☐ MELON	☐ APPLES
☐ LEATHER	☐ PEPPER	☐ OAK	☐ TROPICAL FRUITS
☐ MUSHROOM	☐ MINT	☐ BERRIES	☐ GRASS
☐ JAM	☐ SPICE	☐ NUTMEG	☐ FLORAL
☐ CHOCOLATE	☐ ALMOND	☐ VEGETAL	☐ _____

Taste

☐ DARK FRUITS	☐ EARTH	☐ TOAST	☐ NUTMEG
☐ BERRIES	☐ PEPPER	☐ GRASS	☐ VEGETAL
☐ PLUMS	☐ VANILLA	☐ CITRUS	☐ FLORAL
☐ MUSHROOM	☐ COFFEE	☐ MELON	☐ HONEY
☐ TOBACCO	☐ LICORICE	☐ LYCHEE	☐ PEARS
☐ CHOCOLATE	☐ LEATHER	☐ ALMOND	☐ PEACHES

WINE: _____ Vintage: _____ Producer: _____

Region/Country: _____ Price: _____ Date Tasted: _____

Grape(s): _____

Importer/Distributor: _____ Alcohol % _____

Circle Your Ratings Below

Color/Style: Red White Rose Sparkling Effervescent Fortified

Appearance: Thin Translucent Saturated Opaque

Dry/Sweet Spectrum: Dry 1 2 3 4 5 6 7 8 9 10 Sweet

Body: Light Light-Medium Medium Medium-Full Full

Balance: Unbalanced 1 2 3 4 5 6 7 8 9 10 Balanced

Finish: Short Short-Medium Medium Medium-Long Long

Tasting Experience: Poor 1 2 3 4 5 6 7 8 9 10 Excellent

Price-to-Value Ratio: Poor 1 2 3 4 5 6 7 8 9 10 Excellent

Smell

☐ TOAST	☐ COFFEE	☐ CITRUS	☐ HONEY
☐ TOBACCO	☐ SMOKE	☐ MELON	☐ APPLES
☐ LEATHER	☐ PEPPER	☐ OAK	☐ TROPICAL FRUITS
☐ MUSHROOM	☐ MINT	☐ BERRIES	☐ GRASS
☐ JAM	☐ SPICE	☐ NUTMEG	☐ FLORAL
☐ CHOCOLATE	☐ ALMOND	☐ VEGETAL	☐ _____

Taste

☐ DARK FRUITS	☐ EARTH	☐ TOAST	☐ NUTMEG
☐ BERRIES	☐ PEPPER	☐ GRASS	☐ VEGETAL
☐ PLUMS	☐ VANILLA	☐ CITRUS	☐ FLORAL
☐ MUSHROOM	☐ COFFEE	☐ MELON	☐ HONEY
☐ TOBACCO	☐ LICORICE	☐ LYCHEE	☐ PEARS
☐ CHOCOLATE	☐ LEATHER	☐ ALMOND	☐ PEACHES

WINE: _____ Vintage: _____ Producer: _____

Region/Country: _____ Price: _____ Date Tasted: _____

Grape(s): _____

Importer/Distributor: _____ Alcohol % _____

Circle Your Ratings Below

Color/Style: Red   White   Rose   Sparkling   Effervescent   Fortified
Appearance: Thin   Translucent   Saturated   Opaque
Dry/Sweet Spectrum: Dry   1   2   3   4   5   6   7   8   9   10   Sweet
Body: Light   Light-Medium   Medium   Medium-Full   Full
Balance: Unbalanced   1   2   3   4   5   6   7   8   9   10   Balanced
Finish: Short   Short-Medium   Medium   Medium-Long   Long
Tasting Experience: Poor   1   2   3   4   5   6   7   8   9   10   Excellent
Price-to-Value Ratio: Poor   1   2   3   4   5   6   7   8   9   10   Excellent

Smell

☐ TOAST	☐ COFFEE	☐ CITRUS	☐ HONEY
☐ TOBACCO	☐ SMOKE	☐ MELON	☐ APPLES
☐ LEATHER	☐ PEPPER	☐ OAK	☐ TROPICAL FRUITS
☐ MUSHROOM	☐ MINT	☐ BERRIES	☐ GRASS
☐ JAM	☐ SPICE	☐ NUTMEG	☐ FLORAL
☐ CHOCOLATE	☐ ALMOND	☐ VEGETAL	☐ _____

Taste

☐ DARK FRUITS	☐ EARTH	☐ TOAST	☐ NUTMEG
☐ BERRIES	☐ PEPPER	☐ GRASS	☐ VEGETAL
☐ PLUMS	☐ VANILLA	☐ CITRUS	☐ FLORAL
☐ MUSHROOM	☐ COFFEE	☐ MELON	☐ HONEY
☐ TOBACCO	☐ LICORICE	☐ LYCHEE	☐ PEARS
☐ CHOCOLATE	☐ LEATHER	☐ ALMOND	☐ PEACHES

WINE: _____ Vintage: _____ Producer: _____

Region/Country: _____ Price: _____ Date Tasted: _____

Grape(s): _____

Importer/Distributor: _____ Alcohol % _____

Circle Your Ratings Below

Color/Style: Red   White   Rose   Sparkling   Effervescent   Fortified
Appearance: Thin   Translucent   Saturated   Opaque
Dry/Sweet Spectrum: Dry 1 2 3 4 5 6 7 8 9 10 Sweet
Body: Light   Light-Medium   Medium   Medium-Full   Full
Balance: Unbalanced 1 2 3 4 5 6 7 8 9 10 Balanced
Finish: Short   Short-Medium   Medium   Medium-Long   Long
Tasting Experience: Poor 1 2 3 4 5 6 7 8 9 10 Excellent
Price-to-Value Ratio: Poor 1 2 3 4 5 6 7 8 9 10 Excellent

Smell

☐ TOAST	☐ COFFEE	☐ CITRUS	☐ HONEY
☐ TOBACCO	☐ SMOKE	☐ MELON	☐ APPLES
☐ LEATHER	☐ PEPPER	☐ OAK	☐ TROPICAL FRUITS
☐ MUSHROOM	☐ MINT	☐ BERRIES	☐ GRASS
☐ JAM	☐ SPICE	☐ NUTMEG	☐ FLORAL
☐ CHOCOLATE	☐ ALMOND	☐ VEGETAL	☐ _____

Taste

☐ DARK FRUITS	☐ EARTH	☐ TOAST	☐ NUTMEG
☐ BERRIES	☐ PEPPER	☐ GRASS	☐ VEGETAL
☐ PLUMS	☐ VANILLA	☐ CITRUS	☐ FLORAL
☐ MUSHROOM	☐ COFFEE	☐ MELON	☐ HONEY
☐ TOBACCO	☐ LICORICE	☐ LYCHEE	☐ PEARS
☐ CHOCOLATE	☐ LEATHER	☐ ALMOND	☐ PEACHES

WINE: _____ Vintage: _____ Producer: _____

Region/Country: _____ Price: _____ Date Tasted: _____

Grape(s): _____

Importer/Distributor: _____ Alcohol % _____

Circle Your Ratings Below

Color/Style: Red   White   Rose   Sparkling   Effervescent   Fortified
Appearance: Thin   Translucent   Saturated   Opaque
Dry/Sweet Spectrum: Dry 1 2 3 4 5 6 7 8 9 10 Sweet
Body: Light   Light-Medium   Medium   Medium-Full   Full
Balance: Unbalanced 1 2 3 4 5 6 7 8 9 10 Balanced
Finish: Short   Short-Medium   Medium   Medium-Long   Long
Tasting Experience: Poor 1 2 3 4 5 6 7 8 9 10 Excellent
Price-to-Value Ratio: Poor 1 2 3 4 5 6 7 8 9 10 Excellent

Smell

☐ TOAST	☐ COFFEE	☐ CITRUS	☐ HONEY
☐ TOBACCO	☐ SMOKE	☐ MELON	☐ APPLES
☐ LEATHER	☐ PEPPER	☐ OAK	☐ TROPICAL FRUITS
☐ MUSHROOM	☐ MINT	☐ BERRIES	☐ GRASS
☐ JAM	☐ SPICE	☐ NUTMEG	☐ FLORAL
☐ CHOCOLATE	☐ ALMOND	☐ VEGETAL	☐ _____

Taste

☐ DARK FRUITS	☐ EARTH	☐ TOAST	☐ NUTMEG
☐ BERRIES	☐ PEPPER	☐ GRASS	☐ VEGETAL
☐ PLUMS	☐ VANILLA	☐ CITRUS	☐ FLORAL
☐ MUSHROOM	☐ COFFEE	☐ MELON	☐ HONEY
☐ TOBACCO	☐ LICORICE	☐ LYCHEE	☐ PEARS
☐ CHOCOLATE	☐ LEATHER	☐ ALMOND	☐ PEACHES

WINE: _____ Vintage: _____ Producer: _____

Region/Country: _____ Price: _____ Date Tasted: _____

Grape(s): _____

Importer/Distributor: _____ Alcohol % _____

Circle Your Ratings Below

Color/Style: Red   White   Rose   Sparkling   Effervescent   Fortified
Appearance: Thin   Translucent   Saturated   Opaque
Dry/Sweet Spectrum: Dry 1 2 3 4 5 6 7 8 9 10 Sweet
Body: Light   Light-Medium   Medium   Medium-Full   Full
Balance: Unbalanced 1 2 3 4 5 6 7 8 9 10 Balanced
Finish: Short   Short-Medium   Medium   Medium-Long   Long
Tasting Experience: Poor 1 2 3 4 5 6 7 8 9 10 Excellent
Price-to-Value Ratio: Poor   1 2 3 4 5 6 7 8 9 10 Excellent

Smell

☐ TOAST	☐ COFFEE	☐ CITRUS	☐ HONEY
☐ TOBACCO	☐ SMOKE	☐ MELON	☐ APPLES
☐ LEATHER	☐ PEPPER	☐ OAK	☐ TROPICAL FRUITS
☐ MUSHROOM	☐ MINT	☐ BERRIES	☐ GRASS
☐ JAM	☐ SPICE	☐ NUTMEG	☐ FLORAL
☐ CHOCOLATE	☐ ALMOND	☐ VEGETAL	☐ _____

Taste

☐ DARK FRUITS	☐ EARTH	☐ TOAST	☐ NUTMEG
☐ BERRIES	☐ PEPPER	☐ GRASS	☐ VEGETAL
☐ PLUMS	☐ VANILLA	☐ CITRUS	☐ FLORAL
☐ MUSHROOM	☐ COFFEE	☐ MELON	☐ HONEY
☐ TOBACCO	☐ LICORICE	☐ LYCHEE	☐ PEARS
☐ CHOCOLATE	☐ LEATHER	☐ ALMOND	☐ PEACHES

WINE: _____ Vintage: _____ Producer: _____

Region/Country: _____ Price: _____ Date Tasted: _____

Grape(s): _____

Importer/Distributor: _____ Alcohol % _____

Circle Your Ratings Below

Color/Style: Red White Rose Sparkling Effervescent Fortified
Appearance: Thin Translucent Saturated Opaque
Dry/Sweet Spectrum: Dry 1 2 3 4 5 6 7 8 9 10 Sweet
Body: Light Light-Medium Medium Medium-Full Full
Balance: Unbalanced 1 2 3 4 5 6 7 8 9 10 Balanced
Finish: Short Short-Medium Medium Medium-Long Long
Tasting Experience: Poor 1 2 3 4 5 6 7 8 9 10 Excellent
Price-to-Value Ratio: Poor 1 2 3 4 5 6 7 8 9 10 Excellent

Smell

☐ TOAST	☐ COFFEE	☐ CITRUS	☐ HONEY
☐ TOBACCO	☐ SMOKE	☐ MELON	☐ APPLES
☐ LEATHER	☐ PEPPER	☐ OAK	☐ TROPICAL FRUITS
☐ MUSHROOM	☐ MINT	☐ BERRIES	☐ GRASS
☐ JAM	☐ SPICE	☐ NUTMEG	☐ FLORAL
☐ CHOCOLATE	☐ ALMOND	☐ VEGETAL	☐ _____

Taste

☐ DARK FRUITS	☐ EARTH	☐ TOAST	☐ NUTMEG
☐ BERRIES	☐ PEPPER	☐ GRASS	☐ VEGETAL
☐ PLUMS	☐ VANILLA	☐ CITRUS	☐ FLORAL
☐ MUSHROOM	☐ COFFEE	☐ MELON	☐ HONEY
☐ TOBACCO	☐ LICORICE	☐ LYCHEE	☐ PEARS
☐ CHOCOLATE	☐ LEATHER	☐ ALMOND	☐ PEACHES

WINE: _____ Vintage: _____ Producer: _____

Region/Country: _____ Price: _____ Date Tasted: _____

Grape(s): _____

Importer/Distributor: _____ Alcohol % _____

Circle Your Ratings Below

Color/Style: Red White Rose Sparkling Effervescent Fortified
Appearance: Thin Translucent Saturated Opaque
Dry/Sweet Spectrum: Dry 1 2 3 4 5 6 7 8 9 10 Sweet
Body: Light Light-Medium Medium Medium-Full Full
Balance: Unbalanced 1 2 3 4 5 6 7 8 9 10 Balanced
Finish: Short Short-Medium Medium Medium-Long Long
Tasting Experience: Poor 1 2 3 4 5 6 7 8 9 10 Excellent
Price-to-Value Ratio: Poor 1 2 3 4 5 6 7 8 9 10 Excellent

Smell

☐ TOAST	☐ COFFEE	☐ CITRUS	☐ HONEY
☐ TOBACCO	☐ SMOKE	☐ MELON	☐ APPLES
☐ LEATHER	☐ PEPPER	☐ OAK	☐ TROPICAL FRUITS
☐ MUSHROOM	☐ MINT	☐ BERRIES	☐ GRASS
☐ JAM	☐ SPICE	☐ NUTMEG	☐ FLORAL
☐ CHOCOLATE	☐ ALMOND	☐ VEGETAL	☐ _____

Taste

☐ DARK FRUITS	☐ EARTH	☐ TOAST	☐ NUTMEG
☐ BERRIES	☐ PEPPER	☐ GRASS	☐ VEGETAL
☐ PLUMS	☐ VANILLA	☐ CITRUS	☐ FLORAL
☐ MUSHROOM	☐ COFFEE	☐ MELON	☐ HONEY
☐ TOBACCO	☐ LICORICE	☐ LYCHEE	☐ PEARS
☐ CHOCOLATE	☐ LEATHER	☐ ALMOND	☐ PEACHES

WINE: _____ Vintage: _____ Producer: _____

Region/Country: _____ Price: _____ Date Tasted: _____

Grape(s): _____

Importer/Distributor: _____ Alcohol % _____

Circle Your Ratings Below

Color/Style: Red   White   Rose   Sparkling   Effervescent   Fortified
Appearance: Thin   Translucent   Saturated   Opaque
Dry/Sweet Spectrum: Dry   1   2   3   4   5   6   7   8   9   10   Sweet
Body: Light   Light-Medium   Medium   Medium-Full   Full
Balance: Unbalanced   1 2 3 4 5 6 7 8 9 10   Balanced
Finish: Short   Short-Medium   Medium   Medium-Long   Long
Tasting Experience: Poor   1   2   3   4   5   6   7   8   9   10   Excellent
Price-to-Value Ratio: Poor   1   2   3   4   5   6   7   8   9   10   Excellent

Smell

☐ TOAST	☐ COFFEE	☐ CITRUS	☐ HONEY
☐ TOBACCO	☐ SMOKE	☐ MELON	☐ APPLES
☐ LEATHER	☐ PEPPER	☐ OAK	☐ TROPICAL FRUITS
☐ MUSHROOM	☐ MINT	☐ BERRIES	☐ GRASS
☐ JAM	☐ SPICE	☐ NUTMEG	☐ FLORAL
☐ CHOCOLATE	☐ ALMOND	☐ VEGETAL	☐ _____

Taste

☐ DARK FRUITS	☐ EARTH	☐ TOAST	☐ NUTMEG
☐ BERRIES	☐ PEPPER	☐ GRASS	☐ VEGETAL
☐ PLUMS	☐ VANILLA	☐ CITRUS	☐ FLORAL
☐ MUSHROOM	☐ COFFEE	☐ MELON	☐ HONEY
☐ TOBACCO	☐ LICORICE	☐ LYCHEE	☐ PEARS
☐ CHOCOLATE	☐ LEATHER	☐ ALMOND	☐ PEACHES

WINE: _____ Vintage: _____ Producer: _____

Region/Country: _____ Price: _____ Date Tasted: _____

Grape(s): _____

Importer/Distributor: _____ Alcohol % _____

Circle Your Ratings Below

Color/Style: Red White Rose Sparkling Effervescent Fortified
Appearance: Thin Translucent Saturated Opaque
Dry/Sweet Spectrum: Dry 1 2 3 4 5 6 7 8 9 10 Sweet
Body: Light Light-Medium Medium Medium-Full Full
Balance: Unbalanced 1 2 3 4 5 6 7 8 9 10 Balanced
Finish: Short Short-Medium Medium Medium-Long Long
Tasting Experience: Poor 1 2 3 4 5 6 7 8 9 10 Excellent
Price-to-Value Ratio: Poor 1 2 3 4 5 6 7 8 9 10 Excellent

Smell

☐ TOAST	☐ COFFEE	☐ CITRUS	☐ HONEY
☐ TOBACCO	☐ SMOKE	☐ MELON	☐ APPLES
☐ LEATHER	☐ PEPPER	☐ OAK	☐ TROPICAL FRUITS
☐ MUSHROOM	☐ MINT	☐ BERRIES	☐ GRASS
☐ JAM	☐ SPICE	☐ NUTMEG	☐ FLORAL
☐ CHOCOLATE	☐ ALMOND	☐ VEGETAL	☐ _____

Taste

☐ DARK FRUITS	☐ EARTH	☐ TOAST	☐ NUTMEG
☐ BERRIES	☐ PEPPER	☐ GRASS	☐ VEGETAL
☐ PLUMS	☐ VANILLA	☐ CITRUS	☐ FLORAL
☐ MUSHROOM	☐ COFFEE	☐ MELON	☐ HONEY
☐ TOBACCO	☐ LICORICE	☐ LYCHEE	☐ PEARS
☐ CHOCOLATE	☐ LEATHER	☐ ALMOND	☐ PEACHES

WINE: _____ Vintage: _____ Producer: _____

Region/Country: _____ Price: _____ Date Tasted: _____

Grape(s): _____

Importer/Distributor: _____ Alcohol % _____

Circle Your Ratings Below

Color/Style: Red White Rose Sparkling Effervescent Fortified

Appearance: Thin Translucent Saturated Opaque

Dry/Sweet Spectrum: Dry 1 2 3 4 5 6 7 8 9 10 Sweet

Body: Light Light-Medium Medium Medium-Full Full

Balance: Unbalanced 1 2 3 4 5 6 7 8 9 10 Balanced

Finish: Short Short-Medium Medium Medium-Long Long

Tasting Experience: Poor 1 2 3 4 5 6 7 8 9 10 Excellent

Price-to-Value Ratio: Poor 1 2 3 4 5 6 7 8 9 10 Excellent

Smell

☐ TOAST	☐ COFFEE	☐ CITRUS	☐ HONEY
☐ TOBACCO	☐ SMOKE	☐ MELON	☐ APPLES
☐ LEATHER	☐ PEPPER	☐ OAK	☐ TROPICAL FRUITS
☐ MUSHROOM	☐ MINT	☐ BERRIES	☐ GRASS
☐ JAM	☐ SPICE	☐ NUTMEG	☐ FLORAL
☐ CHOCOLATE	☐ ALMOND	☐ VEGETAL	☐ _____

Taste

☐ DARK FRUITS	☐ EARTH	☐ TOAST	☐ NUTMEG
☐ BERRIES	☐ PEPPER	☐ GRASS	☐ VEGETAL
☐ PLUMS	☐ VANILLA	☐ CITRUS	☐ FLORAL
☐ MUSHROOM	☐ COFFEE	☐ MELON	☐ HONEY
☐ TOBACCO	☐ LICORICE	☐ LYCHEE	☐ PEARS
☐ CHOCOLATE	☐ LEATHER	☐ ALMOND	☐ PEACHES

WINE: _____ Vintage: _____ Producer: _____

Region/Country: _____ Price: _____ Date Tasted: _____

Grape(s): _____

Importer/Distributor: _____ Alcohol % _____

Circle Your Ratings Below

Color/Style: Red   White   Rose   Sparkling   Effervescent   Fortified

Appearance: Thin   Translucent   Saturated   Opaque

Dry/Sweet Spectrum: Dry   1   2   3   4   5   6   7   8   9   10   Sweet

Body: Light   Light-Medium   Medium   Medium-Full   Full

Balance: Unbalanced   1   2   3   4   5   6   7   8   9   10   Balanced

Finish: Short   Short-Medium   Medium   Medium-Long   Long

Tasting Experience: Poor   1   2   3   4   5   6   7   8   9   10   Excellent

Price-to-Value Ratio: Poor   1   2   3   4   5   6   7   8   9   10   Excellent

Smell

☐ TOAST	☐ COFFEE	☐ CITRUS	☐ HONEY
☐ TOBACCO	☐ SMOKE	☐ MELON	☐ APPLES
☐ LEATHER	☐ PEPPER	☐ OAK	☐ TROPICAL FRUITS
☐ MUSHROOM	☐ MINT	☐ BERRIES	☐ GRASS
☐ JAM	☐ SPICE	☐ NUTMEG	☐ FLORAL
☐ CHOCOLATE	☐ ALMOND	☐ VEGETAL	☐ _____

Taste

☐ DARK FRUITS	☐ EARTH	☐ TOAST	☐ NUTMEG
☐ BERRIES	☐ PEPPER	☐ GRASS	☐ VEGETAL
☐ PLUMS	☐ VANILLA	☐ CITRUS	☐ FLORAL
☐ MUSHROOM	☐ COFFEE	☐ MELON	☐ HONEY
☐ TOBACCO	☐ LICORICE	☐ LYCHEE	☐ PEARS
☐ CHOCOLATE	☐ LEATHER	☐ ALMOND	☐ PEACHES

WINE: _____ Vintage: _____ Producer: _____

Region/Country: _____ Price: _____ Date Tasted: _____

Grape(s): _____

Importer/Distributor: _____ Alcohol % _____

Circle Your Ratings Below

Color/Style: Red   White   Rose   Sparkling   Effervescent   Fortified

Appearance: Thin   Translucent   Saturated   Opaque

Dry/Sweet Spectrum: Dry   1 2 3 4 5 6 7 8 9 10   Sweet

Body: Light   Light-Medium   Medium   Medium-Full   Full

Balance: Unbalanced   1 2 3 4 5 6 7 8 9 10   Balanced

Finish: Short   Short-Medium   Medium   Medium-Long   Long

Tasting Experience: Poor   1 2 3 4 5 6 7 8 9 10   Excellent

Price-to-Value Ratio: Poor   1 2 3 4 5 6 7 8 9 10   Excellent

Smell

☐ TOAST	☐ COFFEE	☐ CITRUS	☐ HONEY
☐ TOBACCO	☐ SMOKE	☐ MELON	☐ APPLES
☐ LEATHER	☐ PEPPER	☐ OAK	☐ TROPICAL FRUITS
☐ MUSHROOM	☐ MINT	☐ BERRIES	☐ GRASS
☐ JAM	☐ SPICE	☐ NUTMEG	☐ FLORAL
☐ CHOCOLATE	☐ ALMOND	☐ VEGETAL	☐ _____

Taste

☐ DARK FRUITS	☐ EARTH	☐ TOAST	☐ NUTMEG
☐ BERRIES	☐ PEPPER	☐ GRASS	☐ VEGETAL
☐ PLUMS	☐ VANILLA	☐ CITRUS	☐ FLORAL
☐ MUSHROOM	☐ COFFEE	☐ MELON	☐ HONEY
☐ TOBACCO	☐ LICORICE	☐ LYCHEE	☐ PEARS
☐ CHOCOLATE	☐ LEATHER	☐ ALMOND	☐ PEACHES

WINE: _____ Vintage: _____ Producer: _____

Region/Country: _____ Price: _____ Date Tasted: _____

Grape(s): _____

Importer/Distributor: _____ Alcohol % _____

Circle Your Ratings Below

Color/Style: Red   White   Rose   Sparkling   Effervescent   Fortified
Appearance: Thin   Translucent   Saturated   Opaque
Dry/Sweet Spectrum: Dry 1 2 3 4 5 6 7 8 9 10 Sweet
Body: Light   Light-Medium   Medium   Medium-Full   Full
Balance: Unbalanced 1 2 3 4 5 6 7 8 9 10 Balanced
Finish: Short   Short-Medium   Medium   Medium-Long   Long
Tasting Experience: Poor 1 2 3 4 5 6 7 8 9 10 Excellent
Price-to-Value Ratio: Poor 1 2 3 4 5 6 7 8 9 10 Excellent

Smell

☐ TOAST	☐ COFFEE	☐ CITRUS	☐ HONEY
☐ TOBACCO	☐ SMOKE	☐ MELON	☐ APPLES
☐ LEATHER	☐ PEPPER	☐ OAK	☐ TROPICAL FRUITS
☐ MUSHROOM	☐ MINT	☐ BERRIES	☐ GRASS
☐ JAM	☐ SPICE	☐ NUTMEG	☐ FLORAL
☐ CHOCOLATE	☐ ALMOND	☐ VEGETAL	☐ _____

Taste

☐ DARK FRUITS	☐ EARTH	☐ TOAST	☐ NUTMEG
☐ BERRIES	☐ PEPPER	☐ GRASS	☐ VEGETAL
☐ PLUMS	☐ VANILLA	☐ CITRUS	☐ FLORAL
☐ MUSHROOM	☐ COFFEE	☐ MELON	☐ HONEY
☐ TOBACCO	☐ LICORICE	☐ LYCHEE	☐ PEARS
☐ CHOCOLATE	☐ LEATHER	☐ ALMOND	☐ PEACHES

WINE: _____ Vintage: _____ Producer: _____

Region/Country: _____ Price: _____ Date Tasted: _____

Grape(s): _____

Importer/Distributor: _____ Alcohol % _____

Circle Your Ratings Below

Color/Style: Red   White   Rose   Sparkling   Effervescent   Fortified
Appearance: Thin   Translucent   Saturated   Opaque
Dry/Sweet Spectrum: Dry   1 2 3 4 5 6 7 8 9 10   Sweet
Body: Light   Light-Medium   Medium   Medium-Full   Full
Balance: Unbalanced 1 2 3 4 5 6 7 8 9 10   Balanced
Finish: Short   Short-Medium   Medium   Medium-Long   Long
Tasting Experience: Poor   1 2 3 4 5 6 7 8 9 10   Excellent
Price-to-Value Ratio: Poor   1 2 3 4 5 6 7 8 9 10   Excellent

Smell

☐ TOAST	☐ COFFEE	☐ CITRUS	☐ HONEY
☐ TOBACCO	☐ SMOKE	☐ MELON	☐ APPLES
☐ LEATHER	☐ PEPPER	☐ OAK	☐ TROPICAL FRUITS
☐ MUSHROOM	☐ MINT	☐ BERRIES	☐ GRASS
☐ JAM	☐ SPICE	☐ NUTMEG	☐ FLORAL
☐ CHOCOLATE	☐ ALMOND	☐ VEGETAL	☐ _____

Taste

☐ DARK FRUITS	☐ EARTH	☐ TOAST	☐ NUTMEG
☐ BERRIES	☐ PEPPER	☐ GRASS	☐ VEGETAL
☐ PLUMS	☐ VANILLA	☐ CITRUS	☐ FLORAL
☐ MUSHROOM	☐ COFFEE	☐ MELON	☐ HONEY
☐ TOBACCO	☐ LICORICE	☐ LYCHEE	☐ PEARS
☐ CHOCOLATE	☐ LEATHER	☐ ALMOND	☐ PEACHES

WINE: _____ Vintage: _____ Producer: _____

Region/Country: _____ Price: _____ Date Tasted: _____

Grape(s): _____

Importer/Distributor: _____ Alcohol % _____

Circle Your Ratings Below

Color/Style: Red White Rose Sparkling Effervescent Fortified
Appearance: Thin Translucent Saturated Opaque
Dry/Sweet Spectrum: Dry 1 2 3 4 5 6 7 8 9 10 Sweet
Body: Light Light-Medium Medium Medium-Full Full
Balance: Unbalanced 1 2 3 4 5 6 7 8 9 10 Balanced
Finish: Short Short-Medium Medium Medium-Long Long
Tasting Experience: Poor 1 2 3 4 5 6 7 8 9 10 Excellent
Price-to-Value Ratio: Poor 1 2 3 4 5 6 7 8 9 10 Excellent

Smell

☐ TOAST	☐ COFFEE	☐ CITRUS	☐ HONEY
☐ TOBACCO	☐ SMOKE	☐ MELON	☐ APPLES
☐ LEATHER	☐ PEPPER	☐ OAK	☐ TROPICAL FRUITS
☐ MUSHROOM	☐ MINT	☐ BERRIES	☐ GRASS
☐ JAM	☐ SPICE	☐ NUTMEG	☐ FLORAL
☐ CHOCOLATE	☐ ALMOND	☐ VEGETAL	☐ _____

Taste

☐ DARK FRUITS	☐ EARTH	☐ TOAST	☐ NUTMEG
☐ BERRIES	☐ PEPPER	☐ GRASS	☐ VEGETAL
☐ PLUMS	☐ VANILLA	☐ CITRUS	☐ FLORAL
☐ MUSHROOM	☐ COFFEE	☐ MELON	☐ HONEY
☐ TOBACCO	☐ LICORICE	☐ LYCHEE	☐ PEARS
☐ CHOCOLATE	☐ LEATHER	☐ ALMOND	☐ PEACHES

WINE: _____ Vintage: _____ Producer: _____

Region/Country: _____ Price: _____ Date Tasted: _____

Grape(s): _____

Importer/Distributor: _____ Alcohol % _____

Circle Your Ratings Below

Color/Style: Red   White   Rose   Sparkling   Effervescent   Fortified

Appearance: Thin   Translucent   Saturated   Opaque

Dry/Sweet Spectrum: Dry   1 2 3 4 5 6 7 8 9 10   Sweet

Body: Light   Light-Medium   Medium   Medium-Full   Full

Balance: Unbalanced   1 2 3 4 5 6 7 8 9 10   Balanced

Finish: Short   Short-Medium   Medium   Medium-Long   Long

Tasting Experience: Poor   1 2 3 4 5 6 7 8 9 10   Excellent

Price-to-Value Ratio: Poor   1 2 3 4 5 6 7 8 9 10   Excellent

Smell

☐ TOAST	☐ COFFEE	☐ CITRUS	☐ HONEY
☐ TOBACCO	☐ SMOKE	☐ MELON	☐ APPLES
☐ LEATHER	☐ PEPPER	☐ OAK	☐ TROPICAL FRUITS
☐ MUSHROOM	☐ MINT	☐ BERRIES	☐ GRASS
☐ JAM	☐ SPICE	☐ NUTMEG	☐ FLORAL
☐ CHOCOLATE	☐ ALMOND	☐ VEGETAL	☐ _____

Taste

☐ DARK FRUITS	☐ EARTH	☐ TOAST	☐ NUTMEG
☐ BERRIES	☐ PEPPER	☐ GRASS	☐ VEGETAL
☐ PLUMS	☐ VANILLA	☐ CITRUS	☐ FLORAL
☐ MUSHROOM	☐ COFFEE	☐ MELON	☐ HONEY
☐ TOBACCO	☐ LICORICE	☐ LYCHEE	☐ PEARS
☐ CHOCOLATE	☐ LEATHER	☐ ALMOND	☐ PEACHES

WINE: _____ Vintage: _____ Producer: _____

Region/Country: _____ Price: _____ Date Tasted: _____

Grape(s): _____

Importer/Distributor: _____ Alcohol % _____

Circle Your Ratings Below

Color/Style: Red White Rose Sparkling Effervescent Fortified
Appearance: Thin Translucent Saturated Opaque
Dry/Sweet Spectrum: Dry 1 2 3 4 5 6 7 8 9 10 Sweet
Body: Light Light-Medium Medium Medium-Full Full
Balance: Unbalanced 1 2 3 4 5 6 7 8 9 10 Balanced
Finish: Short Short-Medium Medium Medium-Long Long
Tasting Experience: Poor 1 2 3 4 5 6 7 8 9 10 Excellent
Price-to-Value Ratio: Poor 1 2 3 4 5 6 7 8 9 10 Excellent

Smell

☐ TOAST	☐ COFFEE	☐ CITRUS	☐ HONEY
☐ TOBACCO	☐ SMOKE	☐ MELON	☐ APPLES
☐ LEATHER	☐ PEPPER	☐ OAK	☐ TROPICAL FRUITS
☐ MUSHROOM	☐ MINT	☐ BERRIES	☐ GRASS
☐ JAM	☐ SPICE	☐ NUTMEG	☐ FLORAL
☐ CHOCOLATE	☐ ALMOND	☐ VEGETAL	☐ _____

Taste

☐ DARK FRUITS	☐ EARTH	☐ TOAST	☐ NUTMEG
☐ BERRIES	☐ PEPPER	☐ GRASS	☐ VEGETAL
☐ PLUMS	☐ VANILLA	☐ CITRUS	☐ FLORAL
☐ MUSHROOM	☐ COFFEE	☐ MELON	☐ HONEY
☐ TOBACCO	☐ LICORICE	☐ LYCHEE	☐ PEARS
☐ CHOCOLATE	☐ LEATHER	☐ ALMOND	☐ PEACHES

WINE: _____ Vintage: _____ Producer: _____

Region/Country: _____ Price: _____ Date Tasted: _____

Grape(s): _____

Importer/Distributor: _____ Alcohol % _____

Circle Your Ratings Below

Color/Style: Red   White   Rose   Sparkling   Effervescent   Fortified
Appearance: Thin   Translucent   Saturated   Opaque
Dry/Sweet Spectrum: Dry 1 2 3 4 5 6 7 8 9 10 Sweet
Body: Light   Light-Medium   Medium   Medium-Full   Full
Balance: Unbalanced 1 2 3 4 5 6 7 8 9 10 Balanced
Finish: Short   Short-Medium   Medium   Medium-Long   Long
Tasting Experience: Poor 1 2 3 4 5 6 7 8 9 10 Excellent
Price-to-Value Ratio: Poor 1 2 3 4 5 6 7 8 9 10 Excellent

Smell

☐ TOAST	☐ COFFEE	☐ CITRUS	☐ HONEY
☐ TOBACCO	☐ SMOKE	☐ MELON	☐ APPLES
☐ LEATHER	☐ PEPPER	☐ OAK	☐ TROPICAL FRUITS
☐ MUSHROOM	☐ MINT	☐ BERRIES	☐ GRASS
☐ JAM	☐ SPICE	☐ NUTMEG	☐ FLORAL
☐ CHOCOLATE	☐ ALMOND	☐ VEGETAL	☐ _____

Taste

☐ DARK FRUITS	☐ EARTH	☐ TOAST	☐ NUTMEG
☐ BERRIES	☐ PEPPER	☐ GRASS	☐ VEGETAL
☐ PLUMS	☐ VANILLA	☐ CITRUS	☐ FLORAL
☐ MUSHROOM	☐ COFFEE	☐ MELON	☐ HONEY
☐ TOBACCO	☐ LICORICE	☐ LYCHEE	☐ PEARS
☐ CHOCOLATE	☐ LEATHER	☐ ALMOND	☐ PEACHES

WINE: _____ Vintage: _____ Producer: _____

Region/Country: _____ Price: _____ Date Tasted: _____

Grape(s): _____

Importer/Distributor: _____ Alcohol % _____

Circle Your Ratings Below

Color/Style: Red White Rose Sparkling Effervescent Fortified

Appearance: Thin Translucent Saturated Opaque

Dry/Sweet Spectrum: Dry 1 2 3 4 5 6 7 8 9 10 Sweet

Body: Light Light-Medium Medium Medium-Full Full

Balance: Unbalanced 1 2 3 4 5 6 7 8 9 10 Balanced

Finish: Short Short-Medium Medium Medium-Long Long

Tasting Experience: Poor 1 2 3 4 5 6 7 8 9 10 Excellent

Price-to-Value Ratio: Poor 1 2 3 4 5 6 7 8 9 10 Excellent

Smell

☐ TOAST	☐ COFFEE	☐ CITRUS	☐ HONEY
☐ TOBACCO	☐ SMOKE	☐ MELON	☐ APPLES
☐ LEATHER	☐ PEPPER	☐ OAK	☐ TROPICAL FRUITS
☐ MUSHROOM	☐ MINT	☐ BERRIES	☐ GRASS
☐ JAM	☐ SPICE	☐ NUTMEG	☐ FLORAL
☐ CHOCOLATE	☐ ALMOND	☐ VEGETAL	☐ _____

Taste

☐ DARK FRUITS	☐ EARTH	☐ TOAST	☐ NUTMEG
☐ BERRIES	☐ PEPPER	☐ GRASS	☐ VEGETAL
☐ PLUMS	☐ VANILLA	☐ CITRUS	☐ FLORAL
☐ MUSHROOM	☐ COFFEE	☐ MELON	☐ HONEY
☐ TOBACCO	☐ LICORICE	☐ LYCHEE	☐ PEARS
☐ CHOCOLATE	☐ LEATHER	☐ ALMOND	☐ PEACHES

WINE: _____ Vintage: _____ Producer: _____

Region/Country: _____ Price: _____ Date Tasted: _____

Grape(s): _____

Importer/Distributor: _____ Alcohol % _____

Circle Your Ratings Below

Color/Style: Red   White   Rose   Sparkling   Effervescent   Fortified

Appearance: Thin   Translucent   Saturated   Opaque

Dry/Sweet Spectrum: Dry 1 2 3 4 5 6 7 8 9 10 Sweet

Body: Light   Light-Medium   Medium   Medium-Full   Full

Balance: Unbalanced 1 2 3 4 5 6 7 8 9 10 Balanced

Finish: Short   Short-Medium   Medium   Medium-Long   Long

Tasting Experience: Poor 1 2 3 4 5 6 7 8 9 10 Excellent

Price-to-Value Ratio: Poor 1 2 3 4 5 6 7 8 9 10 Excellent

Smell

☐ TOAST	☐ COFFEE	☐ CITRUS	☐ HONEY
☐ TOBACCO	☐ SMOKE	☐ MELON	☐ APPLES
☐ LEATHER	☐ PEPPER	☐ OAK	☐ TROPICAL FRUITS
☐ MUSHROOM	☐ MINT	☐ BERRIES	☐ GRASS
☐ JAM	☐ SPICE	☐ NUTMEG	☐ FLORAL
☐ CHOCOLATE	☐ ALMOND	☐ VEGETAL	☐ _____

Taste

☐ DARK FRUITS	☐ EARTH	☐ TOAST	☐ NUTMEG
☐ BERRIES	☐ PEPPER	☐ GRASS	☐ VEGETAL
☐ PLUMS	☐ VANILLA	☐ CITRUS	☐ FLORAL
☐ MUSHROOM	☐ COFFEE	☐ MELON	☐ HONEY
☐ TOBACCO	☐ LICORICE	☐ LYCHEE	☐ PEARS
☐ CHOCOLATE	☐ LEATHER	☐ ALMOND	☐ PEACHES

WINE: _____ Vintage: _____ Producer: _____

Region/Country: _____ Price: _____ Date Tasted: _____

Grape(s): _____

Importer/Distributor: _____ Alcohol % _____

Circle Your Ratings Below

Color/Style: Red   White   Rose   Sparkling   Effervescent   Fortified
Appearance: Thin   Translucent   Saturated   Opaque
Dry/Sweet Spectrum: Dry 1 2 3 4 5 6 7 8 9 10 Sweet
Body: Light   Light-Medium   Medium   Medium-Full   Full
Balance: Unbalanced 1 2 3 4 5 6 7 8 9 10 Balanced
Finish: Short   Short-Medium   Medium   Medium-Long   Long
Tasting Experience: Poor   1 2 3 4 5 6 7 8 9 10   Excellent
Price-to-Value Ratio: Poor   1 2 3 4 5 6 7 8 9 10   Excellent

Smell

☐ TOAST	☐ COFFEE	☐ CITRUS	☐ HONEY
☐ TOBACCO	☐ SMOKE	☐ MELON	☐ APPLES
☐ LEATHER	☐ PEPPER	☐ OAK	☐ TROPICAL FRUITS
☐ MUSHROOM	☐ MINT	☐ BERRIES	☐ GRASS
☐ JAM	☐ SPICE	☐ NUTMEG	☐ FLORAL
☐ CHOCOLATE	☐ ALMOND	☐ VEGETAL	☐ _____

Taste

☐ DARK FRUITS	☐ EARTH	☐ TOAST	☐ NUTMEG
☐ BERRIES	☐ PEPPER	☐ GRASS	☐ VEGETAL
☐ PLUMS	☐ VANILLA	☐ CITRUS	☐ FLORAL
☐ MUSHROOM	☐ COFFEE	☐ MELON	☐ HONEY
☐ TOBACCO	☐ LICORICE	☐ LYCHEE	☐ PEARS
☐ CHOCOLATE	☐ LEATHER	☐ ALMOND	☐ PEACHES

WINE: _____ Vintage: _____ Producer: _____

Region/Country: _____ Price: _____ Date Tasted: _____

Grape(s): _____

Importer/Distributor: _____ Alcohol % _____

Circle Your Ratings Below

Color/Style: Red   White   Rose   Sparkling   Effervescent   Fortified
Appearance: Thin   Translucent   Saturated   Opaque
Dry/Sweet Spectrum: Dry   1 2 3 4 5 6 7 8 9 10   Sweet
Body: Light   Light-Medium   Medium   Medium-Full   Full
Balance: Unbalanced   1 2 3 4 5 6 7 8 9 10   Balanced
Finish: Short   Short-Medium   Medium   Medium-Long   Long
Tasting Experience: Poor   1 2 3 4 5 6 7 8 9 10   Excellent
Price-to-Value Ratio: Poor   1 2 3 4 5 6 7 8 9 10   Excellent

Smell

☐ TOAST	☐ COFFEE	☐ CITRUS	☐ HONEY
☐ TOBACCO	☐ SMOKE	☐ MELON	☐ APPLES
☐ LEATHER	☐ PEPPER	☐ OAK	☐ TROPICAL FRUITS
☐ MUSHROOM	☐ MINT	☐ BERRIES	☐ GRASS
☐ JAM	☐ SPICE	☐ NUTMEG	☐ FLORAL
☐ CHOCOLATE	☐ ALMOND	☐ VEGETAL	☐ _____

Taste

☐ DARK FRUITS	☐ EARTH	☐ TOAST	☐ NUTMEG
☐ BERRIES	☐ PEPPER	☐ GRASS	☐ VEGETAL
☐ PLUMS	☐ VANILLA	☐ CITRUS	☐ FLORAL
☐ MUSHROOM	☐ COFFEE	☐ MELON	☐ HONEY
☐ TOBACCO	☐ LICORICE	☐ LYCHEE	☐ PEARS
☐ CHOCOLATE	☐ LEATHER	☐ ALMOND	☐ PEACHES

WINE: _____ Vintage: _____ Producer: _____

Region/Country: _____ Price: _____ Date Tasted: _____

Grape(s): _____

Importer/Distributor: _____ Alcohol % _____

Circle Your Ratings Below

Color/Style: Red   White   Rose   Sparkling   Effervescent   Fortified
Appearance: Thin   Translucent   Saturated   Opaque
Dry/Sweet Spectrum: Dry 1 2 3 4 5 6 7 8 9 10 Sweet
Body: Light   Light-Medium   Medium   Medium-Full   Full
Balance: Unbalanced 1 2 3 4 5 6 7 8 9 10 Balanced
Finish: Short   Short-Medium   Medium   Medium-Long   Long
Tasting Experience: Poor 1 2 3 4 5 6 7 8 9 10 Excellent
Price-to-Value Ratio: Poor 1 2 3 4 5 6 7 8 9 10 Excellent

Smell

☐ TOAST	☐ COFFEE	☐ CITRUS	☐ HONEY
☐ TOBACCO	☐ SMOKE	☐ MELON	☐ APPLES
☐ LEATHER	☐ PEPPER	☐ OAK	☐ TROPICAL FRUITS
☐ MUSHROOM	☐ MINT	☐ BERRIES	☐ GRASS
☐ JAM	☐ SPICE	☐ NUTMEG	☐ FLORAL
☐ CHOCOLATE	☐ ALMOND	☐ VEGETAL	☐ _____

Taste

☐ DARK FRUITS	☐ EARTH	☐ TOAST	☐ NUTMEG
☐ BERRIES	☐ PEPPER	☐ GRASS	☐ VEGETAL
☐ PLUMS	☐ VANILLA	☐ CITRUS	☐ FLORAL
☐ MUSHROOM	☐ COFFEE	☐ MELON	☐ HONEY
☐ TOBACCO	☐ LICORICE	☐ LYCHEE	☐ PEARS
☐ CHOCOLATE	☐ LEATHER	☐ ALMOND	☐ PEACHES

WINE: _____ Vintage: _____ Producer: _____

Region/Country: _____ Price: _____ Date Tasted: _____

Grape(s): _____

Importer/Distributor: _____ Alcohol % _____

Circle Your Ratings Below

Color/Style: Red   White   Rose   Sparkling   Effervescent   Fortified

Appearance: Thin   Translucent   Saturated   Opaque

Dry/Sweet Spectrum: Dry   1 2 3 4 5 6 7 8 9 10   Sweet

Body: Light   Light-Medium   Medium   Medium-Full   Full

Balance: Unbalanced   1 2 3 4 5 6 7 8 9 10   Balanced

Finish: Short   Short-Medium   Medium   Medium-Long   Long

Tasting Experience: Poor   1 2 3 4 5 6 7 8 9 10   Excellent

Price-to-Value Ratio: Poor   1 2 3 4 5 6 7 8 9 10   Excellent

Smell

☐ TOAST	☐ COFFEE	☐ CITRUS	☐ HONEY
☐ TOBACCO	☐ SMOKE	☐ MELON	☐ APPLES
☐ LEATHER	☐ PEPPER	☐ OAK	☐ TROPICAL FRUITS
☐ MUSHROOM	☐ MINT	☐ BERRIES	☐ GRASS
☐ JAM	☐ SPICE	☐ NUTMEG	☐ FLORAL
☐ CHOCOLATE	☐ ALMOND	☐ VEGETAL	☐ _____

Taste

☐ DARK FRUITS	☐ EARTH	☐ TOAST	☐ NUTMEG
☐ BERRIES	☐ PEPPER	☐ GRASS	☐ VEGETAL
☐ PLUMS	☐ VANILLA	☐ CITRUS	☐ FLORAL
☐ MUSHROOM	☐ COFFEE	☐ MELON	☐ HONEY
☐ TOBACCO	☐ LICORICE	☐ LYCHEE	☐ PEARS
☐ CHOCOLATE	☐ LEATHER	☐ ALMOND	☐ PEACHES

WINE: _____ Vintage: _____ Producer: _____

Region/Country: _____ Price: _____ Date Tasted: _____

Grape(s): _____

Importer/Distributor: _____ Alcohol % _____

Circle Your Ratings Below

Color/Style: Red   White   Rose   Sparkling   Effervescent   Fortified

Appearance: Thin   Translucent   Saturated   Opaque

Dry/Sweet Spectrum: Dry 1 2 3 4 5 6 7 8 9 10 Sweet

Body: Light   Light-Medium   Medium   Medium-Full   Full

Balance: Unbalanced 1 2 3 4 5 6 7 8 9 10 Balanced

Finish: Short   Short-Medium   Medium   Medium-Long   Long

Tasting Experience: Poor 1 2 3 4 5 6 7 8 9 10 Excellent

Price-to-Value Ratio: Poor   1 2 3 4 5 6 7 8 9 10 Excellent

Smell

☐ TOAST	☐ COFFEE	☐ CITRUS	☐ HONEY
☐ TOBACCO	☐ SMOKE	☐ MELON	☐ APPLES
☐ LEATHER	☐ PEPPER	☐ OAK	☐ TROPICAL FRUITS
☐ MUSHROOM	☐ MINT	☐ BERRIES	☐ GRASS
☐ JAM	☐ SPICE	☐ NUTMEG	☐ FLORAL
☐ CHOCOLATE	☐ ALMOND	☐ VEGETAL	☐ _____

Taste

☐ DARK FRUITS	☐ EARTH	☐ TOAST	☐ NUTMEG
☐ BERRIES	☐ PEPPER	☐ GRASS	☐ VEGETAL
☐ PLUMS	☐ VANILLA	☐ CITRUS	☐ FLORAL
☐ MUSHROOM	☐ COFFEE	☐ MELON	☐ HONEY
☐ TOBACCO	☐ LICORICE	☐ LYCHEE	☐ PEARS
☐ CHOCOLATE	☐ LEATHER	☐ ALMOND	☐ PEACHES

WINE: _____ Vintage: _____ Producer: _____

Region/Country: _____ Price: _____ Date Tasted: _____

Grape(s): _____

Importer/Distributor: _____ Alcohol % _____

Circle Your Ratings Below

Color/Style: Red   White   Rose   Sparkling   Effervescent   Fortified
Appearance: Thin   Translucent   Saturated   Opaque
Dry/Sweet Spectrum: Dry   1 2 3 4 5 6 7 8 9 10   Sweet
Body: Light   Light-Medium   Medium   Medium-Full   Full
Balance: Unbalanced   1 2 3 4 5 6 7 8 9 10   Balanced
Finish: Short   Short-Medium   Medium   Medium-Long   Long
Tasting Experience: Poor   1 2 3 4 5 6 7 8 9 10   Excellent
Price-to-Value Ratio: Poor   1 2 3 4 5 6 7 8 9 10   Excellent

Smell

☐ TOAST	☐ COFFEE	☐ CITRUS	☐ HONEY
☐ TOBACCO	☐ SMOKE	☐ MELON	☐ APPLES
☐ LEATHER	☐ PEPPER	☐ OAK	☐ TROPICAL FRUITS
☐ MUSHROOM	☐ MINT	☐ BERRIES	☐ GRASS
☐ JAM	☐ SPICE	☐ NUTMEG	☐ FLORAL
☐ CHOCOLATE	☐ ALMOND	☐ VEGETAL	☐ _____

Taste

☐ DARK FRUITS	☐ EARTH	☐ TOAST	☐ NUTMEG
☐ BERRIES	☐ PEPPER	☐ GRASS	☐ VEGETAL
☐ PLUMS	☐ VANILLA	☐ CITRUS	☐ FLORAL
☐ MUSHROOM	☐ COFFEE	☐ MELON	☐ HONEY
☐ TOBACCO	☐ LICORICE	☐ LYCHEE	☐ PEARS
☐ CHOCOLATE	☐ LEATHER	☐ ALMOND	☐ PEACHES

WINE: _____ Vintage: _____ Producer: _____

Region/Country: _____ Price: _____ Date Tasted: _____

Grape(s): _____

Importer/Distributor: _____ Alcohol % _____

Circle Your Ratings Below

Color/Style: Red   White   Rose   Sparkling   Effervescent   Fortified
Appearance: Thin   Translucent   Saturated   Opaque
Dry/Sweet Spectrum: Dry 1 2 3 4 5 6 7 8 9 10 Sweet
Body: Light   Light-Medium   Medium   Medium-Full   Full
Balance: Unbalanced 1 2 3 4 5 6 7 8 9 10 Balanced
Finish: Short   Short-Medium   Medium   Medium-Long   Long
Tasting Experience: Poor   1 2 3 4 5 6 7 8 9 10 Excellent
Price-to-Value Ratio: Poor   1 2 3 4 5 6 7 8 9 10 Excellent

Smell

☐ TOAST	☐ COFFEE	☐ CITRUS	☐ HONEY
☐ TOBACCO	☐ SMOKE	☐ MELON	☐ APPLES
☐ LEATHER	☐ PEPPER	☐ OAK	☐ TROPICAL FRUITS
☐ MUSHROOM	☐ MINT	☐ BERRIES	☐ GRASS
☐ JAM	☐ SPICE	☐ NUTMEG	☐ FLORAL
☐ CHOCOLATE	☐ ALMOND	☐ VEGETAL	☐ _____

Taste

☐ DARK FRUITS	☐ EARTH	☐ TOAST	☐ NUTMEG
☐ BERRIES	☐ PEPPER	☐ GRASS	☐ VEGETAL
☐ PLUMS	☐ VANILLA	☐ CITRUS	☐ FLORAL
☐ MUSHROOM	☐ COFFEE	☐ MELON	☐ HONEY
☐ TOBACCO	☐ LICORICE	☐ LYCHEE	☐ PEARS
☐ CHOCOLATE	☐ LEATHER	☐ ALMOND	☐ PEACHES

WINE: _____ Vintage: _____ Producer: _____

Region/Country: _____ Price: _____ Date Tasted: _____

Grape(s): _____

Importer/Distributor: _____ Alcohol % _____

Circle Your Ratings Below

Color/Style: Red   White   Rose   Sparkling   Effervescent   Fortified
Appearance: Thin   Translucent   Saturated   Opaque
Dry/Sweet Spectrum: Dry   1 2 3 4 5 6 7 8 9 10   Sweet
Body: Light   Light-Medium   Medium   Medium-Full   Full
Balance: Unbalanced   1 2 3 4 5 6 7 8 9 10   Balanced
Finish: Short   Short-Medium   Medium   Medium-Long   Long
Tasting Experience: Poor   1 2 3 4 5 6 7 8 9 10   Excellent
Price-to-Value Ratio: Poor   1 2 3 4 5 6 7 8 9 10   Excellent

Smell

☐ TOAST	☐ COFFEE	☐ CITRUS	☐ HONEY
☐ TOBACCO	☐ SMOKE	☐ MELON	☐ APPLES
☐ LEATHER	☐ PEPPER	☐ OAK	☐ TROPICAL FRUITS
☐ MUSHROOM	☐ MINT	☐ BERRIES	☐ GRASS
☐ JAM	☐ SPICE	☐ NUTMEG	☐ FLORAL
☐ CHOCOLATE	☐ ALMOND	☐ VEGETAL	☐ _____

Taste

☐ DARK FRUITS	☐ EARTH	☐ TOAST	☐ NUTMEG
☐ BERRIES	☐ PEPPER	☐ GRASS	☐ VEGETAL
☐ PLUMS	☐ VANILLA	☐ CITRUS	☐ FLORAL
☐ MUSHROOM	☐ COFFEE	☐ MELON	☐ HONEY
☐ TOBACCO	☐ LICORICE	☐ LYCHEE	☐ PEARS
☐ CHOCOLATE	☐ LEATHER	☐ ALMOND	☐ PEACHES

WINE: _____ Vintage: _____ Producer: _____

Region/Country: _____ Price: _____ Date Tasted: _____

Grape(s): _____

Importer/Distributor: _____ Alcohol % _____

Circle Your Ratings Below

Color/Style: Red   White   Rose   Sparkling   Effervescent   Fortified
Appearance: Thin   Translucent   Saturated   Opaque
Dry/Sweet Spectrum: Dry 1 2 3 4 5 6 7 8 9 10 Sweet
Body: Light   Light-Medium   Medium   Medium-Full   Full
Balance: Unbalanced 1 2 3 4 5 6 7 8 9 10 Balanced
Finish: Short   Short-Medium   Medium   Medium-Long   Long
Tasting Experience: Poor   1 2 3 4 5 6 7 8 9 10   Excellent
Price-to-Value Ratio: Poor   1 2 3 4 5 6 7 8 9 10   Excellent

Smell

☐ TOAST	☐ COFFEE	☐ CITRUS	☐ HONEY
☐ TOBACCO	☐ SMOKE	☐ MELON	☐ APPLES
☐ LEATHER	☐ PEPPER	☐ OAK	☐ TROPICAL FRUITS
☐ MUSHROOM	☐ MINT	☐ BERRIES	☐ GRASS
☐ JAM	☐ SPICE	☐ NUTMEG	☐ FLORAL
☐ CHOCOLATE	☐ ALMOND	☐ VEGETAL	☐ _____

Taste

☐ DARK FRUITS	☐ EARTH	☐ TOAST	☐ NUTMEG
☐ BERRIES	☐ PEPPER	☐ GRASS	☐ VEGETAL
☐ PLUMS	☐ VANILLA	☐ CITRUS	☐ FLORAL
☐ MUSHROOM	☐ COFFEE	☐ MELON	☐ HONEY
☐ TOBACCO	☐ LICORICE	☐ LYCHEE	☐ PEARS
☐ CHOCOLATE	☐ LEATHER	☐ ALMOND	☐ PEACHES

WINE: _____ Vintage: _____ Producer: _____

Region/Country: _____ Price: _____ Date Tasted: _____

Grape(s): _____

Importer/Distributor: _____ Alcohol % _____

Circle Your Ratings Below

Color/Style: Red   White   Rose   Sparkling   Effervescent   Fortified
Appearance: Thin   Translucent   Saturated   Opaque
Dry/Sweet Spectrum: Dry   1 2 3 4 5 6 7 8 9 10   Sweet
Body: Light   Light-Medium   Medium   Medium-Full   Full
Balance: Unbalanced   1 2 3 4 5 6 7 8 9 10   Balanced
Finish: Short   Short-Medium   Medium   Medium-Long   Long
Tasting Experience: Poor   1 2 3 4 5 6 7 8 9 10   Excellent
Price-to-Value Ratio: Poor   1 2 3 4 5 6 7 8 9 10   Excellent

Smell

☐ TOAST	☐ COFFEE	☐ CITRUS	☐ HONEY
☐ TOBACCO	☐ SMOKE	☐ MELON	☐ APPLES
☐ LEATHER	☐ PEPPER	☐ OAK	☐ TROPICAL FRUITS
☐ MUSHROOM	☐ MINT	☐ BERRIES	☐ GRASS
☐ JAM	☐ SPICE	☐ NUTMEG	☐ FLORAL
☐ CHOCOLATE	☐ ALMOND	☐ VEGETAL	☐ _____

Taste

☐ DARK FRUITS	☐ EARTH	☐ TOAST	☐ NUTMEG
☐ BERRIES	☐ PEPPER	☐ GRASS	☐ VEGETAL
☐ PLUMS	☐ VANILLA	☐ CITRUS	☐ FLORAL
☐ MUSHROOM	☐ COFFEE	☐ MELON	☐ HONEY
☐ TOBACCO	☐ LICORICE	☐ LYCHEE	☐ PEARS
☐ CHOCOLATE	☐ LEATHER	☐ ALMOND	☐ PEACHES

WINE: _____ Vintage: _____ Producer: _____

Region/Country: _____ Price: _____ Date Tasted: _____

Grape(s): _____

Importer/Distributor: _____ Alcohol % _____

Circle Your Ratings Below

Color/Style: Red   White   Rose   Sparkling   Effervescent   Fortified

Appearance: Thin   Translucent   Saturated   Opaque

Dry/Sweet Spectrum: Dry 1 2 3 4 5 6 7 8 9 10 Sweet

Body: Light   Light-Medium   Medium   Medium-Full   Full

Balance: Unbalanced 1 2 3 4 5 6 7 8 9 10 Balanced

Finish: Short   Short-Medium   Medium   Medium-Long   Long

Tasting Experience: Poor   1 2 3 4 5 6 7 8 9 10   Excellent

Price-to-Value Ratio: Poor   1 2 3 4 5 6 7 8 9 10   Excellent

Smell

☐ TOAST	☐ COFFEE	☐ CITRUS	☐ HONEY
☐ TOBACCO	☐ SMOKE	☐ MELON	☐ APPLES
☐ LEATHER	☐ PEPPER	☐ OAK	☐ TROPICAL FRUITS
☐ MUSHROOM	☐ MINT	☐ BERRIES	☐ GRASS
☐ JAM	☐ SPICE	☐ NUTMEG	☐ FLORAL
☐ CHOCOLATE	☐ ALMOND	☐ VEGETAL	☐ _____

Taste

☐ DARK FRUITS	☐ EARTH	☐ TOAST	☐ NUTMEG
☐ BERRIES	☐ PEPPER	☐ GRASS	☐ VEGETAL
☐ PLUMS	☐ VANILLA	☐ CITRUS	☐ FLORAL
☐ MUSHROOM	☐ COFFEE	☐ MELON	☐ HONEY
☐ TOBACCO	☐ LICORICE	☐ LYCHEE	☐ PEARS
☐ CHOCOLATE	☐ LEATHER	☐ ALMOND	☐ PEACHES

WINE: _____ Vintage: _____ Producer: _____

Region/Country: _____ Price: _____ Date Tasted: _____

Grape(s): _____

Importer/Distributor: _____ Alcohol % _____

Circle Your Ratings Below

Color/Style: Red   White   Rose   Sparkling   Effervescent   Fortified
Appearance: Thin   Translucent   Saturated   Opaque
Dry/Sweet Spectrum: Dry   1   2   3   4   5   6   7   8   9   10   Sweet
Body: Light   Light-Medium   Medium   Medium-Full   Full
Balance: Unbalanced   1   2   3   4   5   6   7   8   9   10   Balanced
Finish: Short   Short-Medium   Medium   Medium-Long   Long
Tasting Experience: Poor   1   2   3   4   5   6   7   8   9   10   Excellent
Price-to-Value Ratio: Poor   1   2   3   4   5   6   7   8   9   10   Excellent

Smell

☐ TOAST	☐ COFFEE	☐ CITRUS	☐ HONEY
☐ TOBACCO	☐ SMOKE	☐ MELON	☐ APPLES
☐ LEATHER	☐ PEPPER	☐ OAK	☐ TROPICAL FRUITS
☐ MUSHROOM	☐ MINT	☐ BERRIES	☐ GRASS
☐ JAM	☐ SPICE	☐ NUTMEG	☐ FLORAL
☐ CHOCOLATE	☐ ALMOND	☐ VEGETAL	☐ _____

Taste

☐ DARK FRUITS	☐ EARTH	☐ TOAST	☐ NUTMEG
☐ BERRIES	☐ PEPPER	☐ GRASS	☐ VEGETAL
☐ PLUMS	☐ VANILLA	☐ CITRUS	☐ FLORAL
☐ MUSHROOM	☐ COFFEE	☐ MELON	☐ HONEY
☐ TOBACCO	☐ LICORICE	☐ LYCHEE	☐ PEARS
☐ CHOCOLATE	☐ LEATHER	☐ ALMOND	☐ PEACHES

WINE: _____ Vintage: _____ Producer: _____

Region/Country: _____ Price: _____ Date Tasted: _____

Grape(s): _____

Importer/Distributor: _____ Alcohol % _____

Circle Your Ratings Below

Color/Style: Red   White   Rose   Sparkling   Effervescent   Fortified
Appearance: Thin   Translucent   Saturated   Opaque
Dry/Sweet Spectrum: Dry 1 2 3 4 5 6 7 8 9 10 Sweet
Body: Light   Light-Medium   Medium   Medium-Full   Full
Balance: Unbalanced 1 2 3 4 5 6 7 8 9 10 Balanced
Finish: Short   Short-Medium   Medium   Medium-Long   Long
Tasting Experience: Poor 1 2 3 4 5 6 7 8 9 10 Excellent
Price-to-Value Ratio: Poor   1 2 3 4 5 6 7 8 9 10 Excellent

Smell

☐ TOAST	☐ COFFEE	☐ CITRUS	☐ HONEY
☐ TOBACCO	☐ SMOKE	☐ MELON	☐ APPLES
☐ LEATHER	☐ PEPPER	☐ OAK	☐ TROPICAL FRUITS
☐ MUSHROOM	☐ MINT	☐ BERRIES	☐ GRASS
☐ JAM	☐ SPICE	☐ NUTMEG	☐ FLORAL
☐ CHOCOLATE	☐ ALMOND	☐ VEGETAL	☐ _____

Taste

☐ DARK FRUITS	☐ EARTH	☐ TOAST	☐ NUTMEG
☐ BERRIES	☐ PEPPER	☐ GRASS	☐ VEGETAL
☐ PLUMS	☐ VANILLA	☐ CITRUS	☐ FLORAL
☐ MUSHROOM	☐ COFFEE	☐ MELON	☐ HONEY
☐ TOBACCO	☐ LICORICE	☐ LYCHEE	☐ PEARS
☐ CHOCOLATE	☐ LEATHER	☐ ALMOND	☐ PEACHES

WINE: _____ Vintage: _____ Producer: _____

Region/Country: _____ Price: _____ Date Tasted: _____

Grape(s): _____

Importer/Distributor: _____ Alcohol % _____

Circle Your Ratings Below

Color/Style: Red   White   Rose   Sparkling   Effervescent   Fortified
Appearance: Thin   Translucent   Saturated   Opaque
Dry/Sweet Spectrum: Dry 1 2 3 4 5 6 7 8 9 10 Sweet
Body: Light   Light-Medium   Medium   Medium-Full   Full
Balance: Unbalanced 1 2 3 4 5 6 7 8 9 10 Balanced
Finish: Short   Short-Medium   Medium   Medium-Long   Long
Tasting Experience: Poor 1 2 3 4 5 6 7 8 9 10 Excellent
Price-to-Value Ratio: Poor 1 2 3 4 5 6 7 8 9 10 Excellent

Smell

☐ TOAST	☐ COFFEE	☐ CITRUS	☐ HONEY
☐ TOBACCO	☐ SMOKE	☐ MELON	☐ APPLES
☐ LEATHER	☐ PEPPER	☐ OAK	☐ TROPICAL FRUITS
☐ MUSHROOM	☐ MINT	☐ BERRIES	☐ GRASS
☐ JAM	☐ SPICE	☐ NUTMEG	☐ FLORAL
☐ CHOCOLATE	☐ ALMOND	☐ VEGETAL	☐ _____

Taste

☐ DARK FRUITS	☐ EARTH	☐ TOAST	☐ NUTMEG
☐ BERRIES	☐ PEPPER	☐ GRASS	☐ VEGETAL
☐ PLUMS	☐ VANILLA	☐ CITRUS	☐ FLORAL
☐ MUSHROOM	☐ COFFEE	☐ MELON	☐ HONEY
☐ TOBACCO	☐ LICORICE	☐ LYCHEE	☐ PEARS
☐ CHOCOLATE	☐ LEATHER	☐ ALMOND	☐ PEACHES

WINE: _____ Vintage: _____ Producer: _____

Region/Country: _____ Price: _____ Date Tasted: _____

Grape(s): _____

Importer/Distributor: _____ Alcohol % _____

Circle Your Ratings Below

Color/Style: Red   White   Rose   Sparkling   Effervescent   Fortified

Appearance: Thin   Translucent   Saturated   Opaque

Dry/Sweet Spectrum: Dry 1 2 3 4 5 6 7 8 9 10 Sweet

Body: Light   Light-Medium   Medium   Medium-Full   Full

Balance: Unbalanced 1 2 3 4 5 6 7 8 9 10 Balanced

Finish: Short   Short-Medium   Medium   Medium-Long   Long

Tasting Experience: Poor   1 2 3 4 5 6 7 8 9 10   Excellent

Price-to-Value Ratio: Poor   1 2 3 4 5 6 7 8 9 10   Excellent

Smell

☐ TOAST	☐ COFFEE	☐ CITRUS	☐ HONEY
☐ TOBACCO	☐ SMOKE	☐ MELON	☐ APPLES
☐ LEATHER	☐ PEPPER	☐ OAK	☐ TROPICAL FRUITS
☐ MUSHROOM	☐ MINT	☐ BERRIES	☐ GRASS
☐ JAM	☐ SPICE	☐ NUTMEG	☐ FLORAL
☐ CHOCOLATE	☐ ALMOND	☐ VEGETAL	☐ _____

Taste

☐ DARK FRUITS	☐ EARTH	☐ TOAST	☐ NUTMEG
☐ BERRIES	☐ PEPPER	☐ GRASS	☐ VEGETAL
☐ PLUMS	☐ VANILLA	☐ CITRUS	☐ FLORAL
☐ MUSHROOM	☐ COFFEE	☐ MELON	☐ HONEY
☐ TOBACCO	☐ LICORICE	☐ LYCHEE	☐ PEARS
☐ CHOCOLATE	☐ LEATHER	☐ ALMOND	☐ PEACHES

WINE: _____ Vintage: _____ Producer: _____

Region/Country: _____ Price: _____ Date Tasted: _____

Grape(s): _____

Importer/Distributor: _____ Alcohol % _____

Circle Your Ratings Below

Color/Style: Red   White   Rose   Sparkling   Effervescent   Fortified
Appearance: Thin   Translucent   Saturated   Opaque
Dry/Sweet Spectrum: Dry 1 2 3 4 5 6 7 8 9 10 Sweet
Body: Light   Light-Medium   Medium   Medium-Full   Full
Balance: Unbalanced 1 2 3 4 5 6 7 8 9 10 Balanced
Finish: Short   Short-Medium   Medium   Medium-Long   Long
Tasting Experience: Poor 1 2 3 4 5 6 7 8 9 10 Excellent
Price-to-Value Ratio: Poor 1 2 3 4 5 6 7 8 9 10 Excellent

Smell

☐ TOAST	☐ COFFEE	☐ CITRUS	☐ HONEY
☐ TOBACCO	☐ SMOKE	☐ MELON	☐ APPLES
☐ LEATHER	☐ PEPPER	☐ OAK	☐ TROPICAL FRUITS
☐ MUSHROOM	☐ MINT	☐ BERRIES	☐ GRASS
☐ JAM	☐ SPICE	☐ NUTMEG	☐ FLORAL
☐ CHOCOLATE	☐ ALMOND	☐ VEGETAL	☐ _____

Taste

☐ DARK FRUITS	☐ EARTH	☐ TOAST	☐ NUTMEG
☐ BERRIES	☐ PEPPER	☐ GRASS	☐ VEGETAL
☐ PLUMS	☐ VANILLA	☐ CITRUS	☐ FLORAL
☐ MUSHROOM	☐ COFFEE	☐ MELON	☐ HONEY
☐ TOBACCO	☐ LICORICE	☐ LYCHEE	☐ PEARS
☐ CHOCOLATE	☐ LEATHER	☐ ALMOND	☐ PEACHES

WINE: _____ Vintage: _____ Producer: _____

Region/Country: _____ Price: _____ Date Tasted: _____

Grape(s): _____

Importer/Distributor: _____ Alcohol % _____

Circle Your Ratings Below

Color/Style: Red   White   Rose   Sparkling   Effervescent   Fortified
Appearance: Thin   Translucent   Saturated   Opaque
Dry/Sweet Spectrum: Dry 1 2 3 4 5 6 7 8 9 10 Sweet
Body: Light   Light-Medium   Medium   Medium-Full   Full
Balance: Unbalanced 1 2 3 4 5 6 7 8 9 10 Balanced
Finish: Short   Short-Medium   Medium   Medium-Long   Long
Tasting Experience: Poor 1 2 3 4 5 6 7 8 9 10 Excellent
Price-to-Value Ratio: Poor   1 2 3 4 5 6 7 8 9 10 Excellent

Smell

☐ TOAST	☐ COFFEE	☐ CITRUS	☐ HONEY
☐ TOBACCO	☐ SMOKE	☐ MELON	☐ APPLES
☐ LEATHER	☐ PEPPER	☐ OAK	☐ TROPICAL FRUITS
☐ MUSHROOM	☐ MINT	☐ BERRIES	☐ GRASS
☐ JAM	☐ SPICE	☐ NUTMEG	☐ FLORAL
☐ CHOCOLATE	☐ ALMOND	☐ VEGETAL	☐ _____

Taste

☐ DARK FRUITS	☐ EARTH	☐ TOAST	☐ NUTMEG
☐ BERRIES	☐ PEPPER	☐ GRASS	☐ VEGETAL
☐ PLUMS	☐ VANILLA	☐ CITRUS	☐ FLORAL
☐ MUSHROOM	☐ COFFEE	☐ MELON	☐ HONEY
☐ TOBACCO	☐ LICORICE	☐ LYCHEE	☐ PEARS
☐ CHOCOLATE	☐ LEATHER	☐ ALMOND	☐ PEACHES

WINE: _____ Vintage: _____ Producer: _____

Region/Country: _____ Price: _____ Date Tasted: _____

Grape(s): _____

Importer/Distributor: _____ Alcohol % _____

Circle Your Ratings Below

Color/Style: Red   White   Rose   Sparkling   Effervescent   Fortified

Appearance: Thin   Translucent   Saturated   Opaque

Dry/Sweet Spectrum: Dry   1   2   3   4   5   6   7   8   9   10   Sweet

Body: Light   Light-Medium   Medium   Medium-Full   Full

Balance: Unbalanced   1   2   3   4   5   6   7   8   9   10   Balanced

Finish: Short   Short-Medium   Medium   Medium-Long   Long

Tasting Experience: Poor   1   2   3   4   5   6   7   8   9   10   Excellent

Price-to-Value Ratio: Poor   1   2   3   4   5   6   7   8   9   10   Excellent

Smell

☐ TOAST	☐ COFFEE	☐ CITRUS	☐ HONEY
☐ TOBACCO	☐ SMOKE	☐ MELON	☐ APPLES
☐ LEATHER	☐ PEPPER	☐ OAK	☐ TROPICAL FRUITS
☐ MUSHROOM	☐ MINT	☐ BERRIES	☐ GRASS
☐ JAM	☐ SPICE	☐ NUTMEG	☐ FLORAL
☐ CHOCOLATE	☐ ALMOND	☐ VEGETAL	☐ _____

Taste

☐ DARK FRUITS	☐ EARTH	☐ TOAST	☐ NUTMEG
☐ BERRIES	☐ PEPPER	☐ GRASS	☐ VEGETAL
☐ PLUMS	☐ VANILLA	☐ CITRUS	☐ FLORAL
☐ MUSHROOM	☐ COFFEE	☐ MELON	☐ HONEY
☐ TOBACCO	☐ LICORICE	☐ LYCHEE	☐ PEARS
☐ CHOCOLATE	☐ LEATHER	☐ ALMOND	☐ PEACHES

WINE: _____ Vintage: _____ Producer: _____

Region/Country: _____ Price: _____ Date Tasted: _____

Grape(s): _____

Importer/Distributor: _____ Alcohol % _____

Circle Your Ratings Below

Color/Style: Red White Rose Sparkling Effervescent Fortified

Appearance: Thin Translucent Saturated Opaque

Dry/Sweet Spectrum: Dry 1 2 3 4 5 6 7 8 9 10 Sweet

Body: Light Light-Medium Medium Medium-Full Full

Balance: Unbalanced 1 2 3 4 5 6 7 8 9 10 Balanced

Finish: Short Short-Medium Medium Medium-Long Long

Tasting Experience: Poor 1 2 3 4 5 6 7 8 9 10 Excellent

Price-to-Value Ratio: Poor 1 2 3 4 5 6 7 8 9 10 Excellent

Smell

☐ TOAST	☐ COFFEE	☐ CITRUS	☐ HONEY
☐ TOBACCO	☐ SMOKE	☐ MELON	☐ APPLES
☐ LEATHER	☐ PEPPER	☐ OAK	☐ TROPICAL FRUITS
☐ MUSHROOM	☐ MINT	☐ BERRIES	☐ GRASS
☐ JAM	☐ SPICE	☐ NUTMEG	☐ FLORAL
☐ CHOCOLATE	☐ ALMOND	☐ VEGETAL	☐ _____

Taste

☐ DARK FRUITS	☐ EARTH	☐ TOAST	☐ NUTMEG
☐ BERRIES	☐ PEPPER	☐ GRASS	☐ VEGETAL
☐ PLUMS	☐ VANILLA	☐ CITRUS	☐ FLORAL
☐ MUSHROOM	☐ COFFEE	☐ MELON	☐ HONEY
☐ TOBACCO	☐ LICORICE	☐ LYCHEE	☐ PEARS
☐ CHOCOLATE	☐ LEATHER	☐ ALMOND	☐ PEACHES

WINE: _____ Vintage: _____ Producer: _____

Region/Country: _____ Price: _____ Date Tasted: _____

Grape(s): _____

Importer/Distributor: _____ Alcohol % _____

Circle Your Ratings Below

Color/Style: Red   White   Rose   Sparkling   Effervescent   Fortified
Appearance: Thin   Translucent   Saturated   Opaque
Dry/Sweet Spectrum: Dry   1 2 3 4 5 6 7 8 9 10   Sweet
Body: Light   Light-Medium   Medium   Medium-Full   Full
Balance: Unbalanced   1 2 3 4 5 6 7 8 9 10   Balanced
Finish: Short   Short-Medium   Medium   Medium-Long   Long
Tasting Experience: Poor   1 2 3 4 5 6 7 8 9 10   Excellent
Price-to-Value Ratio: Poor   1 2 3 4 5 6 7 8 9 10   Excellent

Smell

☐ TOAST	☐ COFFEE	☐ CITRUS	☐ HONEY
☐ TOBACCO	☐ SMOKE	☐ MELON	☐ APPLES
☐ LEATHER	☐ PEPPER	☐ OAK	☐ TROPICAL FRUITS
☐ MUSHROOM	☐ MINT	☐ BERRIES	☐ GRASS
☐ JAM	☐ SPICE	☐ NUTMEG	☐ FLORAL
☐ CHOCOLATE	☐ ALMOND	☐ VEGETAL	☐ _____

Taste

☐ DARK FRUITS	☐ EARTH	☐ TOAST	☐ NUTMEG
☐ BERRIES	☐ PEPPER	☐ GRASS	☐ VEGETAL
☐ PLUMS	☐ VANILLA	☐ CITRUS	☐ FLORAL
☐ MUSHROOM	☐ COFFEE	☐ MELON	☐ HONEY
☐ TOBACCO	☐ LICORICE	☐ LYCHEE	☐ PEARS
☐ CHOCOLATE	☐ LEATHER	☐ ALMOND	☐ PEACHES

WINE: _____ Vintage: _____ Producer: _____

Region/Country: _____ Price: _____ Date Tasted: _____

Grape(s): _____

Importer/Distributor: _____ Alcohol % _____

Circle Your Ratings Below

Color/Style: Red   White   Rose   Sparkling   Effervescent   Fortified
Appearance: Thin   Translucent   Saturated   Opaque
Dry/Sweet Spectrum: Dry 1 2 3 4 5 6 7 8 9 10 Sweet
Body: Light   Light-Medium   Medium   Medium-Full   Full
Balance: Unbalanced 1 2 3 4 5 6 7 8 9 10 Balanced
Finish: Short   Short-Medium   Medium   Medium-Long   Long
Tasting Experience: Poor 1 2 3 4 5 6 7 8 9 10 Excellent
Price-to-Value Ratio: Poor 1 2 3 4 5 6 7 8 9 10 Excellent

Smell

☐ TOAST	☐ COFFEE	☐ CITRUS	☐ HONEY
☐ TOBACCO	☐ SMOKE	☐ MELON	☐ APPLES
☐ LEATHER	☐ PEPPER	☐ OAK	☐ TROPICAL FRUITS
☐ MUSHROOM	☐ MINT	☐ BERRIES	☐ GRASS
☐ JAM	☐ SPICE	☐ NUTMEG	☐ FLORAL
☐ CHOCOLATE	☐ ALMOND	☐ VEGETAL	☐ _____

Taste

☐ DARK FRUITS	☐ EARTH	☐ TOAST	☐ NUTMEG
☐ BERRIES	☐ PEPPER	☐ GRASS	☐ VEGETAL
☐ PLUMS	☐ VANILLA	☐ CITRUS	☐ FLORAL
☐ MUSHROOM	☐ COFFEE	☐ MELON	☐ HONEY
☐ TOBACCO	☐ LICORICE	☐ LYCHEE	☐ PEARS
☐ CHOCOLATE	☐ LEATHER	☐ ALMOND	☐ PEACHES

WINE: _____ Vintage: _____ Producer: _____

Region/Country: _____ Price: _____ Date Tasted: _____

Grape(s): _____

Importer/Distributor: _____ Alcohol % _____

Circle Your Ratings Below

Color/Style: Red   White   Rose   Sparkling   Effervescent   Fortified
Appearance: Thin   Translucent   Saturated   Opaque
Dry/Sweet Spectrum: Dry 1 2 3 4 5 6 7 8 9 10   Sweet
Body: Light   Light-Medium   Medium   Medium-Full   Full
Balance: Unbalanced 1 2 3 4 5 6 7 8 9 10 Balanced
Finish: Short   Short-Medium   Medium   Medium-Long   Long
Tasting Experience: Poor 1 2 3 4 5 6 7 8 9 10 Excellent
Price-to-Value Ratio: Poor 1 2 3 4 5 6 7 8 9 10 Excellent

Smell

☐ TOAST	☐ COFFEE	☐ CITRUS	☐ HONEY
☐ TOBACCO	☐ SMOKE	☐ MELON	☐ APPLES
☐ LEATHER	☐ PEPPER	☐ OAK	☐ TROPICAL FRUITS
☐ MUSHROOM	☐ MINT	☐ BERRIES	☐ GRASS
☐ JAM	☐ SPICE	☐ NUTMEG	☐ FLORAL
☐ CHOCOLATE	☐ ALMOND	☐ VEGETAL	☐ _____

Taste

☐ DARK FRUITS	☐ EARTH	☐ TOAST	☐ NUTMEG
☐ BERRIES	☐ PEPPER	☐ GRASS	☐ VEGETAL
☐ PLUMS	☐ VANILLA	☐ CITRUS	☐ FLORAL
☐ MUSHROOM	☐ COFFEE	☐ MELON	☐ HONEY
☐ TOBACCO	☐ LICORICE	☐ LYCHEE	☐ PEARS
☐ CHOCOLATE	☐ LEATHER	☐ ALMOND	☐ PEACHES

Circle Your Ratings Below

Color/Style: Red   White   Rose   Sparkling   Effervescent   Fortified
Appearance: Thin   Translucent   Saturated   Opaque
Dry/Sweet Spectrum: Dry   1 2 3 4 5 6 7 8 9 10   Sweet
Body: Light   Light-Medium   Medium   Medium-Full   Full
Balance: Unbalanced   1 2 3 4 5 6 7 8 9 10   Balanced
Finish: Short   Short-Medium   Medium   Medium-Long   Long
Tasting Experience: Poor   1 2 3 4 5 6 7 8 9 10   Excellent
Price-to-Value Ratio: Poor   1 2 3 4 5 6 7 8 9 10   Excellent

Smell

☐ TOAST	☐ COFFEE	☐ CITRUS	☐ HONEY
☐ TOBACCO	☐ SMOKE	☐ MELON	☐ APPLES
☐ LEATHER	☐ PEPPER	☐ OAK	☐ TROPICAL FRUITS
☐ MUSHROOM	☐ MINT	☐ BERRIES	☐ GRASS
☐ JAM	☐ SPICE	☐ NUTMEG	☐ FLORAL
☐ CHOCOLATE	☐ ALMOND	☐ VEGETAL	☐ _____

Taste

☐ DARK FRUITS	☐ EARTH	☐ TOAST	☐ NUTMEG
☐ BERRIES	☐ PEPPER	☐ GRASS	☐ VEGETAL
☐ PLUMS	☐ VANILLA	☐ CITRUS	☐ FLORAL
☐ MUSHROOM	☐ COFFEE	☐ MELON	☐ HONEY
☐ TOBACCO	☐ LICORICE	☐ LYCHEE	☐ PEARS
☐ CHOCOLATE	☐ LEATHER	☐ ALMOND	☐ PEACHES

WINE: _____ Vintage: _____ Producer: _____

Region/Country: _____ Price: _____ Date Tasted: _____

Grape(s): _____

Importer/Distributor: _____ Alcohol % _____

Circle Your Ratings Below

Color/Style: Red   White   Rose   Sparkling   Effervescent   Fortified
Appearance: Thin   Translucent   Saturated   Opaque
Dry/Sweet Spectrum: Dry   1   2   3   4   5   6   7   8   9   10   Sweet
Body: Light   Light-Medium   Medium   Medium-Full   Full
Balance: Unbalanced   1   2   3   4   5   6   7   8   9   10   Balanced
Finish: Short   Short-Medium   Medium   Medium-Long   Long
Tasting Experience: Poor   1   2   3   4   5   6   7   8   9   10   Excellent
Price-to-Value Ratio: Poor   1   2   3   4   5   6   7   8   9   10   Excellent

Smell

☐ TOAST	☐ COFFEE	☐ CITRUS	☐ HONEY
☐ TOBACCO	☐ SMOKE	☐ MELON	☐ APPLES
☐ LEATHER	☐ PEPPER	☐ OAK	☐ TROPICAL FRUITS
☐ MUSHROOM	☐ MINT	☐ BERRIES	☐ GRASS
☐ JAM	☐ SPICE	☐ NUTMEG	☐ FLORAL
☐ CHOCOLATE	☐ ALMOND	☐ VEGETAL	☐ _____

Taste

☐ DARK FRUITS	☐ EARTH	☐ TOAST	☐ NUTMEG
☐ BERRIES	☐ PEPPER	☐ GRASS	☐ VEGETAL
☐ PLUMS	☐ VANILLA	☐ CITRUS	☐ FLORAL
☐ MUSHROOM	☐ COFFEE	☐ MELON	☐ HONEY
☐ TOBACCO	☐ LICORICE	☐ LYCHEE	☐ PEARS
☐ CHOCOLATE	☐ LEATHER	☐ ALMOND	☐ PEACHES

WINE: _____ Vintage: _____ Producer: _____

Region/Country: _____ Price: _____ Date Tasted: _____

Grape(s): _____

Importer/Distributor: _____ Alcohol % _____

Circle Your Ratings Below

Color/Style: Red White Rose Sparkling Effervescent Fortified
Appearance: Thin Translucent Saturated Opaque
Dry/Sweet Spectrum: Dry 1 2 3 4 5 6 7 8 9 10 Sweet
Body: Light Light-Medium Medium Medium-Full Full
Balance: Unbalanced 1 2 3 4 5 6 7 8 9 10 Balanced
Finish: Short Short-Medium Medium Medium-Long Long
Tasting Experience: Poor 1 2 3 4 5 6 7 8 9 10 Excellent
Price-to-Value Ratio: Poor 1 2 3 4 5 6 7 8 9 10 Excellent

Smell

☐ TOAST	☐ COFFEE	☐ CITRUS	☐ HONEY
☐ TOBACCO	☐ SMOKE	☐ MELON	☐ APPLES
☐ LEATHER	☐ PEPPER	☐ OAK	☐ TROPICAL FRUITS
☐ MUSHROOM	☐ MINT	☐ BERRIES	☐ GRASS
☐ JAM	☐ SPICE	☐ NUTMEG	☐ FLORAL
☐ CHOCOLATE	☐ ALMOND	☐ VEGETAL	☐ _____

Taste

☐ DARK FRUITS	☐ EARTH	☐ TOAST	☐ NUTMEG
☐ BERRIES	☐ PEPPER	☐ GRASS	☐ VEGETAL
☐ PLUMS	☐ VANILLA	☐ CITRUS	☐ FLORAL
☐ MUSHROOM	☐ COFFEE	☐ MELON	☐ HONEY
☐ TOBACCO	☐ LICORICE	☐ LYCHEE	☐ PEARS
☐ CHOCOLATE	☐ LEATHER	☐ ALMOND	☐ PEACHES

WINE: _____ Vintage: _____ Producer: _____

Region/Country: _____ Price: _____ Date Tasted: _____

Grape(s): _____

Importer/Distributor: _____ Alcohol % _____

Circle Your Ratings Below

Color/Style: Red White Rose Sparkling Effervescent Fortified
Appearance: Thin Translucent Saturated Opaque
Dry/Sweet Spectrum: Dry 1 2 3 4 5 6 7 8 9 10 Sweet
Body: Light Light-Medium Medium Medium-Full Full
Balance: Unbalanced 1 2 3 4 5 6 7 8 9 10 Balanced
Finish: Short Short-Medium Medium Medium-Long Long
Tasting Experience: Poor 1 2 3 4 5 6 7 8 9 10 Excellent
Price-to-Value Ratio: Poor 1 2 3 4 5 6 7 8 9 10 Excellent

Smell

☐ TOAST	☐ COFFEE	☐ CITRUS	☐ HONEY
☐ TOBACCO	☐ SMOKE	☐ MELON	☐ APPLES
☐ LEATHER	☐ PEPPER	☐ OAK	☐ TROPICAL FRUITS
☐ MUSHROOM	☐ MINT	☐ BERRIES	☐ GRASS
☐ JAM	☐ SPICE	☐ NUTMEG	☐ FLORAL
☐ CHOCOLATE	☐ ALMOND	☐ VEGETAL	☐ _____

Taste

☐ DARK FRUITS	☐ EARTH	☐ TOAST	☐ NUTMEG
☐ BERRIES	☐ PEPPER	☐ GRASS	☐ VEGETAL
☐ PLUMS	☐ VANILLA	☐ CITRUS	☐ FLORAL
☐ MUSHROOM	☐ COFFEE	☐ MELON	☐ HONEY
☐ TOBACCO	☐ LICORICE	☐ LYCHEE	☐ PEARS
☐ CHOCOLATE	☐ LEATHER	☐ ALMOND	☐ PEACHES

WINE: _____ Vintage: _____ Producer: _____

Region/Country: _____ Price: _____ Date Tasted: _____

Grape(s): _____

Importer/Distributor: _____ Alcohol % _____

Circle Your Ratings Below

Color/Style: Red White Rose Sparkling Effervescent Fortified
Appearance: Thin Translucent Saturated Opaque
Dry/Sweet Spectrum: Dry 1 2 3 4 5 6 7 8 9 10 Sweet
Body: Light Light-Medium Medium Medium-Full Full
Balance: Unbalanced 1 2 3 4 5 6 7 8 9 10 Balanced
Finish: Short Short-Medium Medium Medium-Long Long
Tasting Experience: Poor 1 2 3 4 5 6 7 8 9 10 Excellent
Price-to-Value Ratio: Poor 1 2 3 4 5 6 7 8 9 10 Excellent

Smell

☐ TOAST	☐ COFFEE	☐ CITRUS	☐ HONEY
☐ TOBACCO	☐ SMOKE	☐ MELON	☐ APPLES
☐ LEATHER	☐ PEPPER	☐ OAK	☐ TROPICAL FRUITS
☐ MUSHROOM	☐ MINT	☐ BERRIES	☐ GRASS
☐ JAM	☐ SPICE	☐ NUTMEG	☐ FLORAL
☐ CHOCOLATE	☐ ALMOND	☐ VEGETAL	☐ _____

Taste

☐ DARK FRUITS	☐ EARTH	☐ TOAST	☐ NUTMEG
☐ BERRIES	☐ PEPPER	☐ GRASS	☐ VEGETAL
☐ PLUMS	☐ VANILLA	☐ CITRUS	☐ FLORAL
☐ MUSHROOM	☐ COFFEE	☐ MELON	☐ HONEY
☐ TOBACCO	☐ LICORICE	☐ LYCHEE	☐ PEARS
☐ CHOCOLATE	☐ LEATHER	☐ ALMOND	☐ PEACHES

WINE: _____ Vintage: _____ Producer: _____

Region/Country: _____ Price: _____ Date Tasted: _____

Grape(s): _____

Importer/Distributor: _____ Alcohol % _____

Circle Your Ratings Below

Color/Style: Red   White   Rose   Sparkling   Effervescent   Fortified
Appearance: Thin   Translucent   Saturated   Opaque
Dry/Sweet Spectrum: Dry 1 2 3 4 5 6 7 8 9 10 Sweet
Body: Light   Light-Medium   Medium   Medium-Full   Full
Balance: Unbalanced 1 2 3 4 5 6 7 8 9 10 Balanced
Finish: Short   Short-Medium   Medium   Medium-Long   Long
Tasting Experience: Poor 1 2 3 4 5 6 7 8 9 10 Excellent
Price-to-Value Ratio: Poor 1 2 3 4 5 6 7 8 9 10 Excellent

Smell

☐ TOAST	☐ COFFEE	☐ CITRUS	☐ HONEY
☐ TOBACCO	☐ SMOKE	☐ MELON	☐ APPLES
☐ LEATHER	☐ PEPPER	☐ OAK	☐ TROPICAL FRUITS
☐ MUSHROOM	☐ MINT	☐ BERRIES	☐ GRASS
☐ JAM	☐ SPICE	☐ NUTMEG	☐ FLORAL
☐ CHOCOLATE	☐ ALMOND	☐ VEGETAL	☐ _____

Taste

☐ DARK FRUITS	☐ EARTH	☐ TOAST	☐ NUTMEG
☐ BERRIES	☐ PEPPER	☐ GRASS	☐ VEGETAL
☐ PLUMS	☐ VANILLA	☐ CITRUS	☐ FLORAL
☐ MUSHROOM	☐ COFFEE	☐ MELON	☐ HONEY
☐ TOBACCO	☐ LICORICE	☐ LYCHEE	☐ PEARS
☐ CHOCOLATE	☐ LEATHER	☐ ALMOND	☐ PEACHES

WINE: _____ Vintage: _____ Producer: _____

Region/Country: _____ Price: _____ Date Tasted: _____

Grape(s): _____

Importer/Distributor: _____ Alcohol % _____

Circle Your Ratings Below

Color/Style: Red White Rose Sparkling Effervescent Fortified
Appearance: Thin Translucent Saturated Opaque
Dry/Sweet Spectrum: Dry 1 2 3 4 5 6 7 8 9 10 Sweet
Body: Light Light-Medium Medium Medium-Full Full
Balance: Unbalanced 1 2 3 4 5 6 7 8 9 10 Balanced
Finish: Short Short-Medium Medium Medium-Long Long
Tasting Experience: Poor 1 2 3 4 5 6 7 8 9 10 Excellent
Price-to-Value Ratio: Poor 1 2 3 4 5 6 7 8 9 10 Excellent

Smell

☐ TOAST	☐ COFFEE	☐ CITRUS	☐ HONEY
☐ TOBACCO	☐ SMOKE	☐ MELON	☐ APPLES
☐ LEATHER	☐ PEPPER	☐ OAK	☐ TROPICAL FRUITS
☐ MUSHROOM	☐ MINT	☐ BERRIES	☐ GRASS
☐ JAM	☐ SPICE	☐ NUTMEG	☐ FLORAL
☐ CHOCOLATE	☐ ALMOND	☐ VEGETAL	☐ _____

Taste

☐ DARK FRUITS	☐ EARTH	☐ TOAST	☐ NUTMEG
☐ BERRIES	☐ PEPPER	☐ GRASS	☐ VEGETAL
☐ PLUMS	☐ VANILLA	☐ CITRUS	☐ FLORAL
☐ MUSHROOM	☐ COFFEE	☐ MELON	☐ HONEY
☐ TOBACCO	☐ LICORICE	☐ LYCHEE	☐ PEARS
☐ CHOCOLATE	☐ LEATHER	☐ ALMOND	☐ PEACHES

WINE: _____ Vintage: _____ Producer: _____

Region/Country: _____ Price: _____ Date Tasted: _____

Grape(s): _____

Importer/Distributor: _____ Alcohol % _____

Circle Your Ratings Below

Color/Style: Red   White   Rose   Sparkling   Effervescent   Fortified
Appearance: Thin   Translucent   Saturated   Opaque
Dry/Sweet Spectrum: Dry   1 2 3 4 5 6 7 8 9 10   Sweet
Body: Light   Light-Medium   Medium   Medium-Full   Full
Balance: Unbalanced   1 2 3 4 5 6 7 8 9 10   Balanced
Finish: Short   Short-Medium   Medium   Medium-Long   Long
Tasting Experience: Poor   1 2 3 4 5 6 7 8 9 10   Excellent
Price-to-Value Ratio: Poor   1 2 3 4 5 6 7 8 9 10   Excellent

Smell

☐ TOAST	☐ COFFEE	☐ CITRUS	☐ HONEY
☐ TOBACCO	☐ SMOKE	☐ MELON	☐ APPLES
☐ LEATHER	☐ PEPPER	☐ OAK	☐ TROPICAL FRUITS
☐ MUSHROOM	☐ MINT	☐ BERRIES	☐ GRASS
☐ JAM	☐ SPICE	☐ NUTMEG	☐ FLORAL
☐ CHOCOLATE	☐ ALMOND	☐ VEGETAL	☐ _____

Taste

☐ DARK FRUITS	☐ EARTH	☐ TOAST	☐ NUTMEG
☐ BERRIES	☐ PEPPER	☐ GRASS	☐ VEGETAL
☐ PLUMS	☐ VANILLA	☐ CITRUS	☐ FLORAL
☐ MUSHROOM	☐ COFFEE	☐ MELON	☐ HONEY
☐ TOBACCO	☐ LICORICE	☐ LYCHEE	☐ PEARS
☐ CHOCOLATE	☐ LEATHER	☐ ALMOND	☐ PEACHES

Notes

Notes

Notes

Notes

"Wine improves with age. The older I get, the better I like it."

~ Anonymous

59127413R00070

Made in the USA
Columbia, SC
30 May 2019